I0147921

## PRAISE FOR CHRISTOPHER WOODS

"To be passionate about gardens but have wanderlust seems like a curse of mythical proportion. It might turn you into a plant explorer, a landscape photographer or, if you are Christopher Woods, into a horticultural sojourner and writer."

*—THE WASHINGTON POST*

"Whether you are a garden globetrotter or an armchair explorer, this book is definitely one to add to your collection."

*—GARDENS ILLUSTRATED*

"Woods's broad outlook is refreshing. . . . Descriptive essays that discuss thoughtfully, cogently, and often humorously the recurring themes. . . . Highly recommended for anyone interested in modern gardens, garden design, or garden travel."

*—LIBRARY JOURNAL*

"Author Chris Woods worked in top British gardens before moving to the States, where he transformed Chanticleer, and in his safe hands we are transported to these special places to discover what makes them notable. . . . His enthusiasm and warmth carry the reader along and make this the perfect gift for people who love real or armchair garden visiting, at home and abroad."

*—THE TELEGRAPH*

"Woods is uniquely qualified to write a book of such a daunting global scope . . . a long love letter to the planet and its people"

*—MOTHER NATURE NETWORK*

"Most if not all will feel the tug of wanderlust and the gardenlust to explore many of these new and beautiful landscapes."

*—NYBG'S PLANT TALK*

# IN BOTANICAL TIME

## THE EXTRAORDINARY LIFESPANS OF THE WORLD'S OLDEST LIVING PLANTS

**CHRISTOPHER WOODS**

CHELSEA GREEN PUBLISHING
WHITE RIVER JUNCTION, VERMONT
LONDON, UK

First published in 2026 by Chelsea Green Publishing | PO Box 4529 | White River Junction, VT 05001 | West Wing, Somerset House, Strand | London, WC2R 1LA, UK | www.chelseagreen.com
A Division of Rizzoli International Publications, Inc. | 49 West 27th Street | New York, NY 10001 | www.rizzoliusa.com



Publisher: Charles Miers
Deputy Publisher: Matthew Derr
Developmental Editor: Stacee Gravelle Lawrence
Designer: Eva Spring

ISBN 978-1-64502-315-9 (hardcover) | ISBN 978-1-64502-316-6 (ebook)
Library of Congress Control Number: 2025041021 (print)

**Our Commitment to Green Publishing**
Chelsea Green sees publishing as a tool for cultural change and ecological stewardship. We strive to align our book manufacturing practices with our editorial mission and to reduce the impact of our business enterprise in the environment. We print our books using vegetable-based inks whenever possible. This book may cost slightly more because it was printed on paper supplied by Versa from well-managed, FSC®-certified forests and other controlled sources.

Authorized EU representative for product safety and compliance
Mondadori Libri S.p.A. | www.mondadori.it
via Gian Battista Vico 42 | Milan, Italy 20123

Printed in the United States of America.
10 9 8 7 6 5 4 3 2 1 26 27 28 29 30

## CONTENTS

# INTRODUCTION

OUR PLANET EARTH is 4.5 billion years old, plus or minus 50 million years. Luca, an acronym for the last universal common ancestor—a single-celled bacterium-like organism, and the ancestor of all known life on Earth—is estimated to have been born 4.2 billion years ago.

How do we know the earth is 4.5 billion years old? The oldest rocks on Earth are from the Acasta Gneiss Complex of northwestern Canada. Uranium-lead dating places these rocks at 4.02 billion years old. Zircon crystals from the Jack Hills in Western Australia, aged at 4.4 billion years, currently hold the record for the oldest minerals on Earth. And analysis of isotopic ratios in meteorites, particularly using lead-lead dating, indicates the age of the Earth to be around 4.5 billion years.

In botanical time, plant life first emerged on land about 550 million years ago, during the Cambrian Period, around the same time as the first land animals began to emerge. Flowering plants arose more than 300 million years ago—some 50 million years before the rise of the dinosaurs. The plant fossil record is incomplete, no surprise with a 550-million-year chronology, but we are getting very close. (I wander away from live plants in one chapter of this book, "Plants in Stone: The Fossils.")

It is thought that liverworts—along with hornworts and mosses, non-vascular plants (bryophytes)—may be the closest living relatives of the first land plants. These tiny plants, billions of them, transformed our planet, converting carbon dioxide and water into chemical energy and oxygen using light energy from the sun.

This book is about the plants on Earth that have evolved to be the longest lived, with thoughts on how and why. There are four methods for measuring the age of living plants and they are: carbon dating, tree ring analysis, measuring the expansion rate of clonal organisms, and made-up stories.

## CARBON DATING

Carbon dating of plants is used to determine the age of a plant as accurately as possible. It is a method used to measure the amount of decaying radioisotope. Carbon-14, a radioactive isotope of carbon, decreases steadily and at accurately measurable rates. Carbon-14 is ubiquitous in the environment. After it forms high up in the atmosphere, plants breathe it in and animals breathe it out. When living things die, they stop taking in carbon-14 and the amount that is left in their body starts the slow process of radioactive decay. The isotopes of unstable radioactive elements eventually decay into other, more stable elements, in a predictable and precise amount of time called a half-life. The half-life of an element is the amount of time required for exactly half of a quantity of that element to decay.

## TREE RING ANALYSIS

Ed Cook, a climate scientist who specializes in dendrochronology at Columbia University avows, "The only way to truly determine the age of a tree is by dendrochronologically counting the rings—and that requires all rings being present or accounted for." Each ring marks a complete year in the tree's life (usually). Tree rings are taken by collecting a sample with an instrument called an increment borer. The borer extracts a thin strip of wood that goes all the way to the center of the tree. If the borer cannot reach the center, or if the center is nonexistent due to heartwood rotting or plain old age, the sample extracted will not be an accurate measure of the tree's age. But Jonathan Barichivich, a director of research at the Centre National de la Recherche Scientifique (CNRS) in France warns, "If tree rings are a book, then for forty years everyone's just been looking at the cover." So partial samples can, it follows, be used *only* to estimate the age of a tree—this happens with the *Fitzroya cupressoides* mentioned in this book.

The underlying patterns of wide or narrow rings also record year-to-year fluctuations in the growth of trees; trees grow more some years than others. The patterns therefore also reveal weather history in addition to age: a tree's growth rate changes in a predictable pattern throughout the year in response to seasonal climate changes, such as droughts and harsh spring frosts, resulting in visible growth rings. Tree rings also provide information on the rates of change in the environment, and changes in climate over a prolonged period.

## CLONAL EXPANSION

Cloning is the process by which individual organisms with identical genomes reproduce. With plants, organisms produce clones via asexual reproduction: this is called parthenogenesis. A colony or genet is a group of genetically identical individuals that all originated vegetatively, not sexually, from a single ancestor. In plants, an individual in such a population is referred to as a ramet. Clonal colonies are common in many plant species. Although many plants reproduce sexually, through the production of seed, most clonal reproduction occurs by underground stolons or rhizomes. Above ground, these plants most often appear to be distinct individuals, but underground they remain interconnected, one clone.

The Pando is the name given to an area of 106 acres (42.8 hectares) in Utah covered in quaking aspen (*Populus tremuloides*). It appears to be a large grove of 47,000 trees, but the trees are clones of one ancestor, making them all genetically identical, one tree with 47,000 above-ground manifestations.

Another example represented in these pages is King's Lomatia (*Lomatia tasmanica*), endemic to Tasmania and estimated to be 43,600 years old.

An underwater meadow in the Mediterranean Sea of the clonal marine grass *Posidonia oceanica* could be up to 100,000 years of age and possibly 200,000; I discuss its relative, *Posidonia australis*, the largest single organism in the world by area.

Old Tjikko (*Picea abies*) is a 600-year-old Norway spruce. It has been cloning itself in a very harsh environment successfully for an estimated 9,550 years.

## MYTHS AND LEGENDS

Like the children's game of "telephone," where the first player produces a message and whispers it to the ear of the second person down the line and so on, some information about the ages of trees has come down through generations of nearby inhabitants. But just as the statement announced by the last player usually differs significantly from that of the first player in the game, any data provided by "transmission chaining" as we call verbal information passed on from one person to another, so we must take into account how easily information can become corrupted by indirect communication and the unreliability of typical human recollection. These myths are often fascinating, particularly when they give trees personalities or claim to imbue them with mystical energy, but have rarely been proven accurate with science. Nevertheless, they are worth recounting occasionally here as a record of how important certain trees have been to human culture, and often relate directly to modern conservation efforts to preserve not only the species, but the trees' role in our cultures.

For example, the myth that living olive trees are thousands of years old—a popular claim throughout the Mediterranean—is at best romantic fabrication. It pleases us to think that a tree standing before us produced olives also consumed by the ancient Greeks and Romans, the Arabs, or the Turks. Without accurate dendrochronology, however, the age of an "ancient" olive tree is impossible to measure. Olive trees' heartwood rots as they age, making them hollow in the center and therefore impossible to date with a core sample. Scientists have found that it is more likely the gnarled ancient trees glorified by the villages where they appear are actually only a few hundred years old. This does not detract from their beauty of course, even if the claims are untrue. In fact, they add mystery and myth to the beautiful reality and make us notice them: what stories are for.

Many are familiar with the Buddhist story of Gautama achieving enlightenment while sitting under a fig tree (*Ficus religiosa*, or pipal). This Bodhi tree is a major attraction for pilgrims, though most don't realize that Sir Alexander Cunningham planted the tree we see today on the supposed original religious site in 1881. There is considerable doubt as to whether the present tree at Bodh Gaya is even a scion of the original Bodhi tree.

## CLIMATE CHANGE

Climate change is often written off as fraud or fiction by many politicians and many corporations with a financial stake in climate denial. We know the climate is currently changing, however—the trees are recording it all for us with their habits.

Meteorologists recorded that 2024 was the hottest year since record keeping began, in 1880. In 2022 and 2023, Earth saw record increases in carbon dioxide emissions from fossil fuels. The concentration of carbon dioxide in the atmosphere has increased from preindustrial levels in the eighteenth century, at approximately 278 parts per million, to about 420 parts per million today.

Glaciers are melting before our eyes, and habitats for plants are also changing dramatically. Half of the world's mountain glaciers are expected to disappear by the end of this century. As temperatures increase and soil moisture changes, plant and vegetative zones are shifting. Trees are forced to migrate to higher elevations to find cooler, more suitable climates for their survival, but there is only so much fertile real estate on a mountain.

Seas are predicted to rise a foot by 2050, regardless of whether we could even stop emitting carbon globally today.

These various factors raise the question of whether trees can adapt quickly enough to environmental stressors to survive, not having been asked to do it so quickly ever before in the history of plant life on Earth.

## WHY CAN SOME PLANTS LIVE TO SUCH A GREAT AGE?

There is no single answer to why certain species develop what seem to be highly specific—if not seemingly outright bizarre—adaptations for longevity, but evolution through natural selection is the big-picture answer. And natural selection is determined by both environment and genetics.

Interestingly, most of the plants featured in this book grow in very adverse conditions. Not adverse enough to kill them, but enough to slow down their growth considerably. So adapting growth rates to the reality of available energy or nutrient sources seems to be an obvious but astoundingly effective means of survival—probably the one humans would do best to emulate ourselves.

Disturbance phenomena such as droughts, wildfires, and hurricanes, or infestations of bacteria, viruses, and fungi—and of course human impacts—represent the main causes of plant death, either immediate or indirect as natural defenses weaken. Plants have evolved many mechanisms to thwart insect and fungal invasion, few against droughts and wildfires, and none against human impact.

The least fertile sites tend to yield the oldest plants—where life is not easy, you tend to hunker down yourself rather than devote all your energy to procreation every season. Precipitous cliffs harbor thousand-year-old individuals such as the Qilian juniper. Nutrient-poor sites, for instance in deserts, and alkaline mountain sites, produce some of the oldest plants. Take *Welwitschia mirabilis*, which grows in the Namib Desert, where in a good year it may receive 3 inches (7.6 centimeters) of rain. But water in the Namib Desert is not guaranteed: in some years, no rain falls. Yet the biggest Welwitschia plant is estimated to have endured for 1,500 years.

Bristlecone pines grow in the White Mountains of California, a land of bitterly frigid winter temperatures, strong winds, piercing sunlight, low rainfall, short growing seasons, and nutrient-deficient limestone and dolomitic alkaline soils. Growth is slow because of all this, but bristlecone pines are able to survive with only slivers of live growth in a mostly-dead tree. Live wood snakes through the characteristically gnarled gray and white timber to a handful of tufts of waxy green needles and dark purple, bristled cones. Over the years, conditions make the trunks stunted and twisted, their hard wood sculpted by the ripping wind into eroded and fantastic shapes. Matching of dead trees' growth rings with living trees' gives us a 9,000-year-long, august history of the species.

Every living thing is born to die—but some take (much) longer to die than others. In the genome of long-lived plants we find many disease-resistant genes; how these were accumulated over the centuries is a subject of much study.

Other mechanisms associated with longevity are gene duplication—a genetic backup system, and the active work of telomerases. Telomerase is an enzyme found inside cells; it adds short, repetitive "caps" to DNA strands. These caps are called telomeres. Each time a cell divides, the telomeres become frayed and slightly shorter. Eventually, they become so short that the cell can no longer divide successfully, and the cell dies. Long-lived plants may have capabilities that prevent or slow down the fraying of the telomeres, thus contributing to the great age of some.

Aging is a complicated process.

## A PASSION FOR PLANTS

I am now seventy-two years old and have spent most of my life working with plants, first as a gardener and then as a director of several public gardens in the United States. I retired from running gardens ten years ago, but I couldn't let go of my passion for plants. So I started to write books about plants. This is my fourth. My interest has evolved through the process of each, from constructed landscapes to wild places—a personal evolution from a fascination with the man-made to the nature-made.

Whether being old myself qualifies me to write this book or piqued my interest in the topic, I can't truly say. But I believe what has qualified me to be the reader's guide through this topic is my passion for plants. I will continue to wander and wonder.

—Christopher Woods

CHAPTER 1

# ASPEN

*Populus tremuloides*

AGE: 14,000 YEARS

PANDO, IT IS CALLED, with *pando* being the Latin word for "I spread." It is the name for 106 acres (42.8 hectares) of male quaking aspen (*Populus tremuloides*) in the Fremont River Ranger District of the Fishlake National Forest in south-central Utah, in the United States. Pando is a large grove of 47,000 trees—or so it appears—but the trees are actually all clones of one ancestor, therefore genetically identical. As one tree with 47,000 above-ground manifestations, it is technically one of the largest plants on earth.

While each individual tree may only live one hundred years or so, new trees follow quickly, sprouting from the enormous root system. That root system is what qualifies Pando for inclusion in this book, for it is estimated to be 14,000 years old.

The Pando tree was identified as a clone in 1976 by Jerry Kemperman and Burton V. Barnes. As part of his work in the American West, Burt began to examine the trembling aspen southwest of Fish Lake, in the late 1960s and early 1970s. Using aerial photography and morphological differentiation techniques such as pollen production, leaf

**LEFT** Pando, a single aspen clone pf 47,000 trees growing from a single root system, making it one of the largest single living organisms on the planet.

**OVERLEAF** Pando in the Utah winter.

comparisons, and root structure studies, Barnes concluded that the aspen "forest" was a single aspen tree, and quite possibly the world's largest organism.

A large-scale genetic sampling and analysis was published in 2008 by Jennifer DeWoody of the U.S. Forest Service, Carol Rowe, Valerie Hipkins, and Karen Mock of Utah State University, which confirmed previous morphological analysis by Barnes and others, and verified that Pando was in fact a single clonal colony.

Although aspen forests do not burn often, aspen trees are extremely sensitive to fire. A fire intense enough to kill the aspen overstory will stimulate abundant suckering, though some suckers arise after any fire. As many as 50,000 to 100,000 suckers can sprout and grow on a single acre after a fire; there seems to be a collective memory in place, urging Pando to regenerate quickly after fire that has been "learned" sometime in the past fourteen centuries.

Quaking aspen is an exceptionally beautiful tree. The photosynthesizing bark is white and smooth and marked with black scars where lower branches have self-pruned. The leaves are triangular but almost round on mature trees, green above and gray beneath. The leaves are held on long, flat pedicels that are flexible, causing the leaves to flutter, quiver, and tremble in the breeze. Aspen trees have a fast growth rate and can increase in height around 2 feet (60 centimeters) per year.

The leaves turn golden yellow in the fall and are a famous feature of the Rocky Mountains and other parts of the American and Canadian West, where bands of gold sweep down the mountains to clear blue lakes and bright green water meadows.

Pando showing its fall color, which mixes brilliantly with the evergreens that grow up among it.

CHAPTER 2

# BAOBAB

*Adansonia* spp.

AGE: UP TO 2,100 YEARS

THE NAME BAOBAB derives from the Arabic *buhibab*, or "father of many seeds". It is sometimes also referred to by the gender-bending common name "mother of the forest," due to the round and protruding "belly" some species exhibit.

Possibly the oldest baobab tree is an African baobab (*Adansonia digitata*) named the Dorsland Baobab, which is famous for continuing to grow even long after it has fallen over. It is about 2,100 years old, and it grows in Khaudum National Park in Namibia. It's almost 100 feet in girth, and it used to be almost 50 feet tall—before it fell over.

The French botanist Michel Adanson, after whom the genus was named, contended that some baobab specimens were as much as 5,000 years old, although growth rates from rings or from empirical observations suggest that baobab populations appear to be much younger than has generally been believed and only very few trees live to ages over 400 years. However, a group of baobabs growing in northern India were analyzed by using radiocarbon dating: both trees are around 800 years old and are the oldest African baobabs outside Africa. The baobab uses several physical traits to ensure

The Avenue of the Baobabs, a famous road in Morondava, Madagascar.

longevity: the ability to store large thousands of liters of water in their swollen, bottle-shaped trunks to combat drought, bark that's evolved to become resistant to the fires common on the savanna and that's also able to regenerate quickly (making it useful to Indigenous peoples, who strip it for rope and other uses) to close up wounds that could prove fatal to other types of trees, a slow growth rate to accommodate harsh growing conditions, and the ability to sprout new stems that also fuse together into a ring around the central cavity to cycle water and nutrients.

Where did baobabs originate? Until now, the theory was that they came from mainland Africa. But a team of international academics successfully sequenced the genomes of each of the eight baobab species, examining their relationship with one another and concluded that they originated in Madagascar, adding geography to the puzzle.

Madagascar, the world's fourth-largest island, split from Africa around 180 million years ago, and separated from the Indian subcontinent about 90 million years ago. Approximately 90 percent of all plant and animal species found in Madagascar today are endemic, including six species of baobab: *Adansonia grandidieri*, *A. madagascariensis*, *A. perrieri*, *A. rubrostipa*, *A. suarezensis*, and *A. za*. Two other species are no longer native to Madagascar. *Adansonia digitata*'s native range is in the tropics and South Africa, and the South Arabian Peninsula. *Adansonia gregorii* is native to Northwstern Australia and the northwest Northern Territory. The two species made their way to Africa and Australia around 12 million years ago, well after the separation of Gondwana; baobab seeds may have been carried across the ocean on floating debris.

Only one baobab species is not included in the International Union for Conservation of Nature

The remarkable flower of the baobab, edible and used to flavor traditional drinks by some Indigenous peoples.

(IUCN) Red List of Threatened Species: *A. digitata*. Three species in Madagascar are threatened with extinction, and one, *A. suarezensis*, is close to becoming critically endangered. Climate modeling indicates the species could become extinct within fifty years without intensive conservation efforts.

The range of the baobab species has been shrinking on the island for millennia, with human-caused climate change and ongoing deforestation exacerbating the shrinkage and fragmentation of baobab populations in recent decades.

Baobabs are accustomed to arid lands; however, Southern Madagascar is experiencing its worst drought in forty years and this, along with rampant deforestation and general habitat loss, means Madagascar's baobabs are in an accelerated struggle for survival.

Baobabs growing on the savanna of a wildlife management area in Tanzania.

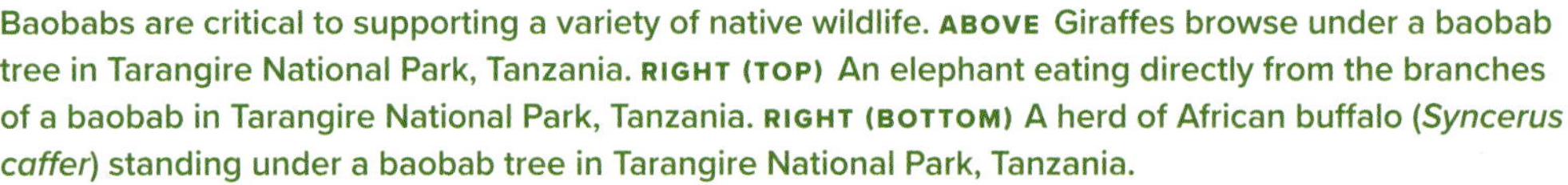

Baobabs are critical to supporting a variety of native wildlife. **ABOVE** Giraffes browse under a baobab tree in Tarangire National Park, Tanzania. **RIGHT (TOP)** An elephant eating directly from the branches of a baobab in Tarangire National Park, Tanzania. **RIGHT (BOTTOM)** A herd of African buffalo (*Syncerus caffer*) standing under a baobab tree in Tarangire National Park, Tanzania.

**LEFT** Unlike many hardwood trees, baobabs are able to survive even when their bark is stripped, as here, by an elephant. **ABOVE (TOP)** Baobab tree bark being twisted into sturdy rope by the Dogon people, who live in the central plateau region of Mali. **ABOVE (LEFT)** Weaver birds make nests in the high, safe branches of baobabs. **ABOVE (RIGHT)** The Dorsland Baobab in Khaudum National Park, Namibia, which has fallen over but continues to grow new stems, leaf out, and bloom.

CHAPTER 3

# BLACK RIVER CYPRESS

*Taxodium distichum*

AGE: 2,624 YEARS

SWAMP CYPRESSES grow in some of Earth's wettest places, and the oldest tree in Eastern North America, at least 2,624 years old, grows in the earthsoup of the Three Sisters cove of the Black River Preserve in North Carolina, U.S. The river is formed by the meeting of the Coharie and Six Runs Creeks, and snakes into the Cape Fear River. It is acidic, tannic, nutrient-poor—and yet full of life.

The Black River cypress is the oldest known living tree in eastern North America, and the fifth-oldest known continuously living, sexually reproducing, nonclonal tree species. It's also the oldest-known wetland tree species in the world.

*Taxodium distichum* is a deciduous conifer. It typically grows to heights of 35 to 120 feet (10 to 40 meters) and has a trunk diameter of 3 to 6 feet (0.9 to 1.8 m). The bark is grayish brown to reddish brown and has an interwoven pattern of shallow grooves and furrows. The needle-like leaves are ½ to ¾ inch (1.3 to 1.9 cm) long. The growth rate, particularly in low-nutrient swamps is slow, greatly

Caddo Lake, in eastern Texas, is home to the world's largest bald cypress forest.

adding to the longevity of the tree. In the fall, the needles turn yellow or copper red. They drop completely each winter, giving the species one of its common names: the "bald" cypress.

The National Champion Bald Cypress, on Cat Island near St. Francisville, Louisiana, is recognized as the largest member of its species in the country. It is 96 feet (29 meters) tall, 56 feet (17 meters) in circumference, and is estimated to be approximately 1,500 years old.

"Big Dan" is one of the oldest living specimens; it grows near High Springs, Florida, at Camp Kulaqua. In 2020, it was is estimated to be over 2,000 years old. It grows in the Hornsby Spring swamp run and is more than 35 feet (10.6 meters) in circumference.

Ancient bald cypress trees tower along the Black River. David Stahle, a professor of geosciences at the University of Arkansas, avows: "We've studied the bald cypress . . . throughout its native range in Latin America and the U.S. This is the best stand we ever found." Stahle's team took out core samples from trees in the area, and used both dendrochronology and carbon dating to determine age. "We have cored and dated only a hundred and ten living bald cypress at this site, but that's a small fraction of the tens of thousands of trees still present in these wetlands. There could well be several additional individual bald cypresses over two thousand years old along the approximately sixty-mile reach of the Black River."

Tree rings not only tell time but record climatic history, too. In warm, wet years, when trees grow

A pristine stand of bald cypress trees along Fisheating Creek, near Palmdale, Florida.

well, the rings are wider, while in drought years, the rings are narrow. The 2,624-year-old bald cypress alone has now extended the paleoclimate record of the Black River region by some 970 years.

"The oldest trees in eastern North America also record one of the most accurate tree-ring records of growing season rainfall ever found," Stahle says. "It's a remarkable discovery, and it's also a wonder that any individual organism can live so long. And when you add to the fact that the annual rings record the history of the environment, it's a tremendous record."

Dendroclimatic reconstructions of rainfall based on Black River and other bald cypress chronologies from the region have revealed decade-long droughts and periods of increased rainfall during Colonial and Precolonial times that exceed any measured during the modern period, including the severe droughts that impacted the first English attempts to settle in America at the Roanoke Island and Jamestown colonies.

"Doctor Stahle's original work on the Black River, which showed trees dating to what Europeans think of as Roman times, inspired us to begin conservation there more than two decades ago," says Katherine Skinner, executive director of The Nature Conservancy's North Carolina chapter. "This ancient forest gives us an idea of what much of North Carolina's coastal plain must have looked like millennia before."

Cypress is known for the brilliant russet red of its fall needles; these trees live at Lake Sukko, near the Black Sea.

Bald cypress is the oldest-known wetland tree species on earth. Only individual trees of Sierra juniper (*Juniperus occidentalis*) at 2,675 years, giant sequoia (*Sequoiadendron giganteum*) at 3,266, alerce (*Fitzroya cupressoides*) at 3,622, and Great Basin bristlecone pine (*Pinus longaeva*) at 5,066 years old are known to live longer than Black River cypress.

Nutrient-poor wetlands may be consistent with a model of "longevity under adversity." The adverse low pH, limited nutrients, and frequently flooded conditions at Black River not only exclude most bottomland hardwood tree species, they are also associated with extremely slow growth rates of bald cypress on this black water stream. The species has also evolved rot-resistant wood, which serves it well in the swamp as well as in general.

The survival of ancient bald cypress and other tree species at Black River provides qualitative and quantitative evidence for the ecological integrity of this wetland ecosystem, however. Qualitatively, an excursion on the Black River where clear tea-colored water flows over white sand and among columnar trees of great age is a unique experience and certainly qualifies this stream as one of the great natural areas of eastern North America.

Quantitatively, the minimum age determinations of selected old-growth bald cypress trees are based on dendrochronology. The habitat value of the Black River is further documented by the high surface water quality, the presence of rare and endangered species, and the recent observations of

Some of the bald cypresses at Caddo Lake in Texas are estimated to be 400 years old.

threatened wood storks (*Mycteria americana*) and swallow-tailed kites (*Elanoides forficatus*).

You can rent a canoe and glide through the Three Sisters Swamp. You'll see trees flat-topped from storms and hollow from rot, standing so still in dark water, and you'll inhale the smell of swamp and Spanish moss. Bobcats, river otters, and black bears also call it home, along with songbirds, warblers, and vireos. Swamp roses bloom in the spring, and spider lilies flower in the summer.

The maximum longevity of wetland tree species has not been well documented. The oldest known are at Black River, but Montezuma bald cypress (*Taxodium mucronatum*) in the 1,200-to-1,500-year age class have been reported in Mexico.

El Árbol del Tule is a massive Montezuma bald cypress that is growing 6 miles (9 kilometers) east of the city of Oaxaca. In 2005, its trunk circumference was 137.8 feet (42.0 meters), equating to a diameter of 46.1 feet (14.05 meters). Its common name, *ahuehuete*, means "old man of the water." Its exact age is unknown, with estimates ranging between 1,200 and 3,000 years. The best scientific estimate based on growth rates is 1,433 to 1,600 years. Local Zapotec legend holds that it was planted about 1,400 years ago by a priest of the Aztec wind god Ehecatl, an aspect of the Feathered Serpent deity Quetzalcoatl.

Unfortunately, the wind god has not been paying it enough attention since—the Oaxacan cypress is now dying from pollution produced by nearby city traffic and compaction from the feet of thousands of tourists who walk around this magnificent tree.

The Árbol de Tule, in Santa Maria del Tule, Oaxaca, Mexico, is a Montezuma cypress, or *ahuehuete* in Nahuatl, and has a trunk circumference of nearly 145 feet; it's estimated to be between 1,400 and 3,000 years old.

CHAPTER 4

# BRISTLECONE PINE

*Pinus aristata, P. longaeva, P. balfouriana*
AGE 4,800+ YEARS

THE FICTIONAL AND mythological Methuselah was a patriarch in Judaism, Christianity, and Islam. It is claimed he lived for 969 years. The myths tell us he was the great-great-great-great-grandson of Seth, the child of Adam and Eve, and grandfather of the mythical Noah. Methuselah has since become a synonym for great age and that brings us to the wooden Methuselah: a bristlecone pine.

There are three species of bristlecone pine, and all are long-lived. One species, *Pinus longaeva*, the Great Basin bristlecone pine, is the longest-lived of all, and the individual named Methuselah, its age verified by tree rings, is more than 4,800 years old.

Methusaleh lives in the Ancient Bristlecone Pine Forest of the White Mountains in Inyo County, in eastern California, U.S. It is a land of bitterly frigid winter temperatures, strong winds, piercing sunlight, low rainfall, short growing seasons, and nutrient-deficient limestone and dolomitic alkaline soils. Growth is slow because of it. Daunting as the harsh environment is, it is this environment that is

An ancient *Pinus longaeva* in the Ancient Bristlecone Pine Forest in the White Mountains of California.

the major contributing reason for the longevity of the species. There are other factors, too.

Bristlecone pines are able to live with only slivers of live growth inside the trunk, while most of the tree dies around these live channels. Live wood snakes through the gray and white gnarled timber to a handful of tufts of waxy green needles and dark purple bristled cones. These ancient trees are gnarled, stunted, and twisted by extreme conditions, their hard wood sculpted by the ripping wind into eroded and fantastic shapes. Matching of dead trees' growth rings with living trees' gives us a 9,000-year-long record of the species. Each tree, living or dead, records the gravity of history.

*The beauty of the tree is not how old,*
*Indeed how ancient in its gnarling now,*
*Not in its silent history yet untold,*
*Nor in the pre-historic roots and bough—*
*Their age—but in its newness ever new,*
*Its torqued refusal to be caught by death,*
*Rejection of defeat enclasped in screw-*
*Shaped trunk, five-thousand-year eon's breath*
*There in its arid air, determined bark,*
*Those needles prickly and the feisty cones*
*Which stand against, aghast, against the stark*
*Realities which beat against its bones,*
*These needles and these cones forever young,*
*Which sing forever like a new-made tongue.*

PHILLIP WHIDDEN

The gnarled roots of this *Pinus longaeva* speak to the harshness of its environment in the Inyo National Forest, California.

The Rocky Mountain bristlecone pine, *Pinus aristata*, is also long-lived. The oldest tree in Colorado, in Pike National Forest, is 2,465 years old. On Mount Goliath "Great Grandma" has been dated back to 403 CE, making it 2,062 years old. As with *Pinus longaeva*, the oldest Rocky Mountain bristlecone pines occur on high-elevation, dry sites that promote slow rates of tree growth and delay heart rot decay. A dozen Rocky Mountain bristlecone pines in the South Park area of Colorado are documented as being over 1,600 years of age.

*Pinus aristata* grows to 49 to 66 feet (15 to 20 meters) tall, with single but occasionally multiple trunks with white-gray bark on young trees, which becomes red brown to gray and scaly on old trees. Growth is varied depending on elevation. It is a small tree at upper subalpine elevations. On low-elevation sites it often reaches 40 feet (12 meters) in height and 30 inches (75 centimeters) in circumference. Branches of younger trees are low and reach upward, forming a dense, spreading, conical crown. Old trees become beautifully irregular, with vertical ribbons of dead wood, many dead branches, and crown dieback. The needles are dark green in color, often spotted with white resin. The seed cones are dark purple turning brown and are tipped with a thin bristle.

**ABOVE** The cones of *Pinus aristata* are remarkable for their dark purple color and thin bristle tip.

**LEFT** A *Pinus aristata* in the Mount Evans Wilderness of Colorado.

Rocky Mountain bristlecone pine communities are varied. Some grow in pure groves, while others grow in stands mixed with Engelmann spruce (*Picea engelmannii*), subalpine fir (*Abies lasiocarpa*), lodgepole pine (*Pinus contorta*), and limber pine (*Pinus flexilis*).

Mount Blue Sky (formerly Mount Evans) is about 51 miles (82 kilometers) by road from Denver, Colorado. It is 14,266.1 feet (4,348 meters) high, and it is one of the best places to walk among Rocky Mountain bristlecone pines.

A summer hike down walking trails alongside snow-melt streams will take you through stands of bristlecones, blue spruce (*Picea pungens*), and quaking aspen (*Populus tremuloides*). Mountain flowers are plentiful and beautiful. White and blue Rocky Mountain columbine (*Aquilegia saxi-montana*) grows with alpine forget-me-not (*Eritrichium nanum*), alpine sandwort (*Cherleria obtusiloba*), moss campion (*Silene acaulis*), alpine phlox (*Phlox condensata*), and fairy primrose (*Primula angustifolia*). Hiking Mount Blue Sky is one of the best things a human can experience in terms of mountain botany.

A grove of *Pinus aristata* growing at the timberline (11,000 feet) in the Mount Evans Wildnerness of Colorado.

The foxtail pine (*Pinus balfouriana*) is the third bristlecone. It is not as common as the other two species. It grows at the treeline in the Klamath and Sierra Mountains, with two subspecies, northern (subsp. *balfouriana*) and southern (subsp. *austrina*). The oldest foxtail pine on record is a 3,400-year-old southern foxtail pine. Northern foxtail pines occur in wetter habitats than southern foxtail pines and are shorter lived, attaining maximum ages of about 1,600 years.

Foxtail pines are so named because the needles are bunched up together at the end of the branches and resemble (with a little imagination) the fluffy tail of a fox. It is a short pine, only about 45 feet (13.7 meters) tall at its highest. Often it is shorter, stunted and contorted. Its needles are deep glossy green on the outer face, and white on the inner face. The cones are up to 4.5 inches (11 centimeters) long, and dark purple turning red-brown, with soft, flexible scales, each with a central bristle.

If there is one plant that qualifies as the icon of any and all things measured in botanical time, I still vote for the first discussed here: the Great Basin bristlecone pine, Methusaleh.

As Matt Haig appreciates in *How to Stop Time*, "It has been alive since the pharaohs. It has been alive since the founding of Troy. Since the start of the Bronze Age. Since the start of yoga. Since mammoths. And it has stayed there, calmly in its spot, growing slowly, producing leaves, losing leaves, producing more, as those mammoths became extinct . . . the tree has always been the tree."

A foxtail pine, *Pinus balfouriana*, so called for the way its needles clump into tufts.

CHAPTER 5

# CREOSOTE BUSH

*Larrea tridentata*

AGE: 11,700 YEARS

IF YOU HAVE EVER BEEN to the Mojave Desert in monsoon season and watched the silver-black columns of rain march toward you, and then you have raised your face to the sky and breathed in the perfume of the desert rain—the earthy scent of petrichor, that sweet fragrance of anise, sagebrush and the smoky scent of tar, then you have certainly experienced creosote bush.

Creosote bush gains it name from the resinous, tarry odor of its leaves. The Spanish word for the plant, *hediondilla*, means "little stinker." It produces a wide range of compounds that protect it from damage by insects and fungi as well as from being eaten by animals. For example, an antioxidant compound called nordihydroguiaretic acid (NGDA) is present on the leaf surfaces. This and other resinous compounds prevent digestion of the leaf tissues in most animals' guts. Jackrabbits are the only mammals known to really eat the leaves. There are, however, more than sixty insects associated

Creosote bushes grow happily straight out of sand dunes in the Amargosa Range, which runs along the eastern side of California's Death Valley.

with creosote bush, including twenty-two species of bee that feed only on its flowers, and a creosote katydid and creosote grasshopper that use it as a food source. The flowers are also confectionery for the chuckwalla lizard, desert iguana, and several other herbivorous reptiles.

*Larrea tridentata* is an evergreen shrub 3 to 9 feet (1 to 3 meters) high. The leaves are opposite with two asymmetrical leaflets measuring around .39 inches (1 centimeter) in length. The leaves are glossy, with a thick resinous coating secreted by a glandular skin. The stem is woody, and knotty. The flowers are borne solitary in the axils, with five yellow flowers. The fruit is a roundish capsule, covered with a dense concentration of white hair.

Creosote bush is highly drought tolerant. It can live for at least two years with no water at all—by shedding its leaves if necessary, and even shedding branches. The extreme drought tolerance of the leaves is due to a couple of main factors: the leaves are small with a low surface area for water loss, and the leaf cuticle is very thick and waxy.

Creosote lives in the Mojave, Sonoran, and Chihuahuan Deserts of North America and can be found in southeastern California, Arizona, southern Nevada, and Utah, as well as New Mexico and Texas. In Mexico it can be found in the states of Chihuahua, Sonora, Coahuila, Nuevo Leon, Zacatecas, Durango, and San Luis Potosi.

Creosote bush is remarkable in that individual plants live an extremely long time, often 100 to 200 years. But they produce even longer-lived clonal colonies over a period of many centuries, as new shoots are continually produced from the outer edge of the root crown, as the older stems die in the

*Larrea tridentata* is remarkable in that it produces fruit covered by white hairs, but can also reproduce clonally.

center. The result is that these plants gradually move outward—a growing, circular clone.

One of the oldest living organisms on earth is the King Clone creosote ring in the Mojave Desert. This colony has been estimated to have been alive for around 11,700 years. This single clonal colony plant reaches up to 67 feet (20 meters) in diameter.

King Clone was identified and the age estimated by Frank Vasek, a professor at the University of California, Riverside. After Vasek hypothesized that the creosote ring was, in fact, one organism, Leonel da Silveira Lobo O'Reilly Sternberg (then a graduate student working in Vasek's lab), documented that the plants within one ring had more similar characteristics than those from other plant clusters. Vasek then used two methods to estimate the age of the ring. One method counted rings and measured the distance of annual growth, and the other used radiocarbon dating on pieces of wood found in the center of the ring, combined with measuring their distances from each other and the living bushes.

For a scrawny plant that looks like it is suffering a slow starvation on the desert floor, the creosote is, in fact, a champion of survival according to Vasek's findings published in the *American Journal of Botany*. "The oldest we found, dubbed King Clone, is 11,700 years old by our estimates," Vasek said. "We believe it was one of the first life-forms to colonize the Mojave Desert when the last glacier receded and has been a continuous resident there since."

In the Anza-Borrego Desert, creosote bush grows alongside colorful blooms of desert sand verbena (*Abronia villosa* var. *villosa*) and dune evening promises (*Oenothera deltoides* subsp. *deltoides*).

Twenty-two species of bee feed only on the flowers of creosote bush.

But proving his theory became a detective story, because the inside wood and therefore the growth record had long since rotted away. Vasek had to determine if all the bushes in a ring were genetically the same. If they were, the age of that single individual could be estimated by the rate of growth of the plant outward from the center.

It's easy to forget just how remarkable and fascinating this common, unassuming plant really is.

Creosote bush can survive for two years without any precipitation; here in the Amargosa Range, they receive between just 2 and 6 inches per year.

CHAPTER 6

# DRAGON TREE

*Dracaena draco*

AGE: 800 TO 1,000 YEARS

DRAGONS HAVE LONG BEEN associated with earthly phenomenon, and this tree is inextricable from human mythology, which associates medicinal power with its most unique characteristic.

In Egyptian mythology, Apep, a giant serpent, was the enemy of the sun god, Ra. Apep was associated with the dark underworld. The sun set at night and rose in the morning when Ra battled with Apep. It was also said that storms were caused by Apep's battles with Set, the god of storms.

In China, dragons were known for summoning rain—this made them benevolent deities helping to bring prosperity to the land. Chinese dragons also governed other natural elements that are associated with rain: clouds, mist, thunder, and lightning.

Dragon's blood has been endowed with magical properties across cultures. A sword dipped in dragon's blood would cause a wound to never heal; dragon blood gave a person the ability to see into the future; in Wagner's *The Ring*, when Siegfried withdraws his sword from the dragon Fafner's body, tasting the blood granted him the ability to understand the song of the birds of the forest.

The "Millennial" dragon tree, growing in Tenerife, Spain; its age is disputed though all agree its stature is impressive.

And according to Greek myth, Landon, the hundred-headed dragon, guardian of the Garden of the Hesperides, was killed by Hercules while he attempted to bring back three golden apples. Landon's red blood flowed out upon the land and from it sprung up the trees we know today as "Dragon Trees."

Which came first, the legend or the knowledge that certain trees leach red sap? Either way, it's convenient that these trees offer something so astounding, so unlike anything else found in the natural world, it could only be ascribed to myth. This magical substance can be obtained from palms in the genus *Calamus*, from padauk wood in the genus *Pterocarpus*, and particularly from *Dracaena*, a genus of 120 trees and succulent shrubs. Both *D. cinnabari*, native to the island of Socotra, in Yemen, and *D. draco*, native to the Canary Islands and Morocco, have blood-red sap. For centuries, cultures that have come into contact with Dracaena have extracted the sap into a useful resin.

Dragon's blood resin has been used as a dye, a pigment for painting, and for medicine. As a dye, it was used as a varnish by eighteenth-century violin makers in Europe and in China, it was used as a red varnish for furniture. Artists used it to produce flesh tones in paintings—specifically the color known as "Chinese orange." As a medicine, it was used for general wound healing, curing diarrhea, and for lowering fevers. This was long before penicillin. Today, it is still touted by "wellness" companies as incense to clear away stagnant or negative energies, to cleanse a person from sin, and to protect against psychic intrusions. The oldest and largest dragon

An iconic *Dracaena draco* at Mirador de los Dragos, La Palma, Canary Islands, Spain.

The fruit and leaves of a *Dracaena draco* growing in Hawaii.

tree grows in Tenerife, in the Canary Islands. It is estimated to be from 800 to 1,000 years old, and grows in the aptly named Parque del Drago, Icod de los Vinos. Its age is disputed, but its size is not. It is around 66 to 69 feet (20 to 21 meters) tall, with a circumference around 66 feet (20 meters). It has over 300 main branches. When it flowers, it reveals around 1,800 flowering branches, with spikes of fragrant white flowers followed by coral-red berries.

Like all mature dragon plants, it has an umbrella-like look due to its many-pronged branches.

The age of 1,000 years is questioned simply because the problem with calculating the age of dragon trees is that they lack growth rings. They are monocots in the asparagus family (Asparagaceae). They do not produce heartwood; the trunks consist of a fibrous and spongy tissue. In addition, new layers of bark grow from top to bottom, a process so

The layered bark of *Dracaena draco*, with its characteristic red resin seeping through.

slow that it is imperceptible. Two methods are used to calculate the age: counting the number of blooms that have occurred throughout the life of the tree (an average of one flowering occurs every fifteen years, although in the case of wild specimens, the time between floral periods could be much longer than that), and counting of the number of branches. Both methods are considered valid for dragon trees that are between 200 and 300 years old, but some authors do not consider them reliable for those specimens that are over 500 years old, since the blooms become more irregular the older the dragon tree is. If the method of counting the occurrences of blooming on the dragon tree in the Drago de Icod de los Vinos, with a total of 23 recorded, the resulting age would be 360 to 400 years.

As columnist Álvaro Fajardo points out, "Regarding his age, it is true that there is some controversy. The level of disagreement is such that the scientific community is divided. While a group of experts . . . attribute it an approximate age of six hundred and fifty years, based on the theory of floral periods, at the other extreme are those who place it close to two thousand years, supported by the theory of measurement-evolution of stem roots. The truth is that it is hard to believe that this presence, with its dazzling stamp, does not enclose at least a thousand

Since dragon trees grow very slowly but do not have trunks with rings, counting branches becomes another method of determining age.

years . . . it is disconcerting that it is the Canarian scientists themselves who lower the age of the tree."

In any case, and if science does not clarify this matter, this iconic dragon tree will continue to be known as "millenary," a nickname more than earned for its appearance and—who knows—perhaps also for its age. Forestry engineer Juan Guzmán Ojeda says, "What we can say is that this mythological being, the most voluminous of its species, will continue to be, and rightly so, the most famous 'forest beast,' visited and admired by locals and foreigners in this and other corners of the world."

**TOP (LEFT)** A dragon tree growing among cultivated crops north of La Palma, Canary Islands. **TOP (RIGHT)** The *Dracaena* genus is actually a member of the Asparagaceae family, with spongy trunks. **BOTTOM (LEFT)** Due to their slow growth habit, it's possible for dragon trees to survive and thrive in the most unlikely conditions. **BOTTOM (RIGHT)** Dragon trees' bark grows in layers from the top down.

CHAMAECYPARIS
OBTUSA NANA GRACILIS
± 140 ANS
CYPRÈS DU JAPON

CHAPTER 7

# FIVE SACRED TREES OF JAPAN

*Chamaecyparis obtusa, Chamaecyparis pisifera, Cryptomeria japonica, Sciadopitys verticillata, Thujopsis dolabrata*
AGE: 700 TO 7,000 YEARS

THE JAPANESE NAME for *Sciadopitys verticillata* is kōya maki, in reference to Koya Mountain in Wakayama Prefecture on the western coast of the Kii Peninsula, on the Kii Channel, which connects the Pacific Ocean and the Seto Inland Sea. We know it in the West as the umbrella pine.

There are five "sacred" trees in Japan and kōya maki is one. The others are *Cryptomeria japonica*, commonly known as sugi; *Chamaecyparis obtusa*, or hinoki cypress; *Chamaecyparis pisifera*, commonly called sawara; and *Thujopsis dolabrata*, or asunaro.

In the Feudal Era, the five sacred trees in the Kiso Valley were prohibited from logging by the common people with a punishment of decapitation—they were reserved for the elite. Shinto shrines were largely built with wood from the five, as were government buildings and bathtubs. Umbrella pine

A 140-year old Hinoki cypress trained into bonsai form in a Japanese classical garden.

**ABOVE** A kōya maki, Japanese umbrella pine (*Sciadopitys verticillata*).

**RIGHT** *Jizo bosatsu* statues, a five-tiered stupa, and a memorial gravestone all venerate a giant sugi tree in Wakayama Prefecture, Japan.

was often used for boat building and its latex sap for caulking.

Umbrella pine is not a true pine but the sole member of the Sciadopityaceae family. However, it is a spire-like coniferous evergreen with long green, needlelike "leaves" that occur in whorls resembling the spokes of an umbrella. These "leaves" are stem tissue rather than leaf tissue, and are referred to as cladodes—flattened shoot systems that take on the photosynthetic functions of the tree. The true leaves are small, brown, scale-like growths found along the shoot. It is an elegant, slow-growing tree with reddish-brown bark that peels off in strips.

*Sciadopitys* grows in mixed conifer-broadleaf cloud forests with high rainfall and humidity. It grows with hinoki (*Chamaecyparis obtusa*), Japanese hemlock (*Tsuga sieboldii*), momi fir (*Abies firma*), Japanese white pine (*Pinus parviflora*), cucumber tree (*Magnolia obovata*), katsura (*Cercidiphyllum japonicum*) and Honshū maple (*Acer rufinerve*). *Sciadopitys* occurs as scattered individuals, in small groves, or in pure stands, depending on the stage of the forest. It can be seen clothing the slopes of the Daikō Mountain Range, its dark green skirts whirling and spiraling to the sky.

A living fossil with ancestors going back some 230 million years, *Sciadopitys* is an ancient endemic with a prehistoric range in Eurasia and North America. It was already in decline by the time other "ancient" conifers became widespread.

**ABOVE** A sacred asunaro tree (*Thujopsis dolabrata* var. *hondai*) in Aomori.

**LEFT** The expressive branches of *Chamaecyparis obtusa* 'Rashahiba'.

**OPPOSITE (TOP LEFT)** Sawara cypress cones (*Chamaecyparis pisifera* 'Filifera'). **(TOP RIGHT)** Sake being poured in a traditional cypress box drinking vessel. **(BOTTOM)** *Cryptomeria japonica* is so valuable it's often grown in plantations in Japan, as here.

The largest and oldest known specimen is a tree at Jinguji Temple, Nodagawa, Kyoto Prefecture, and is 88 feet (27 meters) tall and has a girth of 13 feet (4 meters). Kyoto Nature describes it: "A tree with origins obscured in the distant past, historical records show that it has been worshipped locally since 1310, when a monk from Ishiyama-dera Temple renovated this temple located in the Ishikawa region and named it Jinguji. Legend says the principal Buddhist image of the temple is a woman, which is why people attending the annual festival touch the umbrella pine—in hopes of being blessed with healthy children. The umbrella pine of Junguji Temple has been designated as a natural monument of Kyoto Prefecture."

*Cryptomeria japonica*, or sugi, can grow into very large specimens of up to 230 feet (70 meters) tall. The evergreen needlelike leaves are arranged spirally. The cones are globular. The bark is red-brown and peels in vertical strips. It is related to giant sequoia (*Sequoiadendron giganteum*) and the genus *Taxodium*.

In instances where the tree has been damaged by weather or human negligence, specimens may produce two or more trunks, often with elephantine branches curving to the ground and then upward to the light. The large branches are often bare, with the foliage appearing in mops at the end.

Sugi is a living fossil, too, in that fossil records show its ancestors go back 230 million years. It has

**ABOVE** Immature cones on a Japanese cedar (*Cryptomeria japonica*); this evergreen is actually botanically related to yews, despite its common name.

**LEFT** A five-story pagoda constructed with and surrounded by sugi trees at Mount Haguro, Dewa Province, Japan.

been a forest plantation tree in Japan for hundreds of years. Its wood is very fragrant and weather-and-insect resistant, so it is widely used for building houses. It is also the national tree of Japan.

Jōmon Sugi is the largest and likely oldest living *Cryptomeria*. It's located on Yakushima, one of the Ōsumi Islands in Kagoshima Prefecture. It is estimated to be between 700 or 2,170 (and sometimes up to 7,200) years old, which is quite a spread. Tree-ring dating conducted by Japanese scientists on the tree's branches indicated that it is at least 2,000 years old. Its exact age is a bit of a mystery. It is found at an elevation of 4,300 feet (1,300 meters), and accessible from a hiking path that takes four to five hours to climb. Accessibility is restricted to protect it from the ravages of foot traffic. It has been described as "a grim titan of a tree, rising from the spongy ground more like rock than timber, his vast muscular arms extended above the tangle of young cedars and camphor trees" by Thomas Pakenham. It is 83 feet (25.3 meters) high, with a trunk circumference of 54 feet (16.4 meters). A titan. Jōmon Sugi is "partnered" with Tāne Mahuta (an *Agathis australis*) in New Zealand's Waipoua Forest, much as sister cities select each other.

*Chamaecyparis obtusa*, or hinoki cypress, is native to central Japan, and is widespread throughout the country. It may reach 115 feet (35 meters) tall with a trunk up to 3 feet (1 meter) in diameter. The bark is a rich, dark red-brown. The leaves are flat and scalelike, opaque green above and below with white

**ABOVE** The scale-like branches of *Chamaecyparis obtusa* 'Nana Gracilis'.

**LEFT** Jōmon Sugi, the largest and purportedly oldest living *Cryptomeria*.

**OVERLEAF** A venerated cedar, Tako Sugi, on the mountain in Takao.

**ABOVE** The wooden floors at Nijo Castle in Kyoto, designed on the underside with special nails that squeak to emit a birdlike noise that sounded like nightingales when walked upon, to alert residents of intruders.

**RIGHT** An ancient *Chamaecyparis obtusa*.

at the base of each scale-leaf. The cones are globose. Its timber is of very high quality and is lemon-scented and pale golden. It is used for the small boxes known as *masu*, into which sake is traditionally poured. The hinoki grown in Kiso are called *go-shin-boku*, or "divine trees."

A 700-year-old hinoki tree can be found at the Daichi-ji Temple in Gifu Prefecture, in the center of the country. Remnants of a 2,800-to-3,000-year-old tree, recovered from a wetland north of Hiroshima, indicates that hinoki can grow to a great age if left to live in peace. The very oldest trees have historically been harvested in great numbers to provide wood to build palaces and temples. Nijo Castle in Kyoto, completed in 1626, for example, was the home of shoguns, the military dictators of Japan from 1185 to 1868. The castle was built as a residence; however, to protect the shogun from enemies, special floorboards were installed to warn residents of intruders. Those floorboards, called nightingale floors, were made from the straight-grained hinoki and the darker and wavy-grained sawara (*Chamaecyparis pisifera*). When walked upon, the floors emit a fluting sound, reminiscent of the song of the Japanese bush warbler, or uguisu, a common songbird in Japan. The floors were designed so that the flooring nails rubbed against a jacket or clamp, causing chirping noises. They were built as security devices; none could come near the shogun without being detected.

**ABOVE** An allée of sugi trees (*Cryptomeria japonica*) in Rikugien Garden.

**RIGHT** Tight cones of umbrella pine (*Sciadopitys verticillata*).

**OPPOSITE (TOP LEFT)** Traditional buckets made of sawara cypress, at the Kinkaku-ji Temple in Kyoto. **(TOP RIGHT)** A hinoki cypress (*Chamaecyparis obtusa*) growing wild in the Tanzawa Mountains. **(BOTTOM)** Honored cypresses at the Nikkō Futarasan shrine, established in the eighth century.

本社境内第一の巨杉
御神木
樹齢　約七百年
太さ　六、三五メートル
高さ　約六〇メートル

**ABOVE** The expressively curled needles of the sawara cypress.

**LEFT** A grove of tall sawara cypresses (*Chamaecyparis pisifera*).

*Chamaecyparis pisifera* is a slow-growing conifer with branches arranged in two opposite, horizontally spreading rows. The branchlets are flat. The leaves are dark green above, green at the tips beneath, but with a broad patch of blue bloom at the base of each. It can reach a height of 150 feet (45 meters). It was, and still is, grown for timber in Japan, and its main traditional use is to make the frame of shoji screens. The oldest living sawara is estimated to be around 800 years old, which given that it is only an estimate, one can take with a drop of sake.

*Thujopsis dolabrata*, or asunaro, reaches up to 131 feet (40 meters) and features red-brown bark that peels in strips. It is the only member of its genus and is in the cypress family (Cupressaceae). It is somewhat like arborvitae (*Thuja*), but differs in having thicker, fleshy, intersecting leaves with vivid white bands underneath. The brown cones are covered in violet-white wax when new.

Asunaro is widely planted around temples, and one, in Toshimi, in Hiroshima Prefecture, is estimated to be about 250 years old. The wood of asunaro has an earthy scent. Its light, soft, durable grain is the wooden basis of much traditional lacquer work. The laquer coating, urushi, is made from the sap harvested from the species *Toxicodendron vernicifluum*.

CHAPTER 8

# GRAN ABUELO

*Fitzroya cupressoides*

AGE: 3,600 TO 5,500 YEARS, OR MORE

OVER 3,600 OR POSSIBLY 5,500 YEARS AGO, (more on that later), a seed from a female cone of the alerce tree fluttered into a crevice in a cold, wet valley in the southern Andes. The winged seed germinated, and the great-grandfather tree, or Gran Abuelo, came to life. It is the second-oldest tree in the world and, with more research, may be revealed to be the oldest—possibly even older than Methusaleh, the 4,856-year-old bristlecone pine, or its relative Prometheus, often estimated to be 4,900 years old (before being cut down in 1964, but still the longest-lived tree definitively documented).

Alerce, Spanish for larch, is actually a misnomer—larch is in the pine family (Pinaceae), but *Fitzroya cupressoides* is the single member of the genus in the cypress family (Cupressaceae). Fitzroya is named after Vice-Admiral Robert FitzRoy (July 5, 1805–April 30, 1865), who was captain of the HMS Beagle during Charles Darwin's great voyage.

Fitzroya is a conical conifer with evergreen needles in crossed whorls of three. The thick bark

The Los Alerces waterfall on the Manso River in Chile, lined by larches, coihues, and *Fitzroya cupressoides*.

peels in longitudinal strips. The wood is reddish-brown. It can reach a height of 150 feet (45 meters). One-third of Chile's forests were burned or cleared by 1955, but *Fitzroya cupressoides* became protected in 1976. Of course, illegal logging still occurs.

Parque Nacional Alerce Costero (Alerce Costero National Park) is part of the Valdivian temperate forest, an ecoregion between the Pacific Ocean and the Andes that hosts not only dense stands of Fitzroya but coihue (*Nothofagus dombeyi*), Chilean hazel (*Gevuina avellana*), white-flowered ulmo (*Eucryphia cordifolia*), the Guaitecas cypress (*Pilgerodendron uviferum*), *Podocarpus nubigenus*, and *Fuchsia magellanica*. Pehuén (*Araucaria araucana*) also grows in substantial numbers in the higher elevations of the park. In the Fitzroya forest, it's interesting that its accompanying tree species are mainly all evergreen broadleafs: *Nothofagus nitida*, *Nothofagus betuloides*, *Drimys winteri*, *Metrosideros stipularis*, *Embothrium coccineum*, and *Weinmannia trichosperma*.

Aníbal Henríquez, the park's first warden, just happened upon the Gran Abuelo in the early 1970s. He kept the find secret, but word got out and soon thousands came to see the great tree every summer. With damage from footfalls and vandalism, the path

**RIGHT** Two different towering alerce trees (*Fitzroya cupressoides*) in Alerce Andino National Park, Chile, which protects over 97,000 acres of temperate rainforest.

to the tree is now closed indefinitely. Climate scientist Jonathan Barichivich grew up in Alerce Costero National Park and has studied the ancient tree. In January 2020, he visited the Gran Abuelo with dendrochronologist Antonio Lara, to take a core sample from the trunk. The trunk is over 13 feet (4.3 meters) wide, and they were able to reach only 40 percent of the way into its. Its center is rotten, making a complete core sample truly unattainable. Yet even the partial sample yielded a finding of about 2,400 years. Barichivich went further, devising a model that could estimate the age. With known ages of other *Fitzroya* nearby, and factoring in climate data, he created a model that created a range of potential ages; he estimates there is an 80 percent chance this tree has lived for more than 5,000 years.

It is a controversial estimate, with some scientists asserting that only a complete and countable tree-ring capable of determining age. It is to be hoped that, soon, the exact age of Gran Abuelo will be decided. If that never comes to fruition, we can still appreciate it for being a grand and ancient tree, a great-grandfather. We bow.

"The Gran Abuelo isn't just old, it's a time capsule with a message about the future," Barichivich says. "We have a five-thousand-year record of life in this tree alone, and we can see the response of an ancient being to the changes we have made to the planet."

Cross-sections of Patagonian cypress trunks, revealing growth rings that substantiate claims of extreme longevity.

RESUCITÓ. ALELUYA...

**LEFT** A cabin built with alerce wood in Pumalín Douglas Tompkins National Park, Chile.

**LEFT (BELOW)** The baroque interior of a UNESCO World Heritage church on Quinchao Island, Chile, originally constructed in 1880 with alerce, canelo, and avellano trees.

**BELOW** The interior of the Church of San Francisco on Chiloé Island, Chile. It was built in 1902 in the style of a Gothic stone church, but using the island's traditional wood craftsmanship and alerce, coihue, and other native woods. It was designated a UNESCO World Heritage Site in 2000.

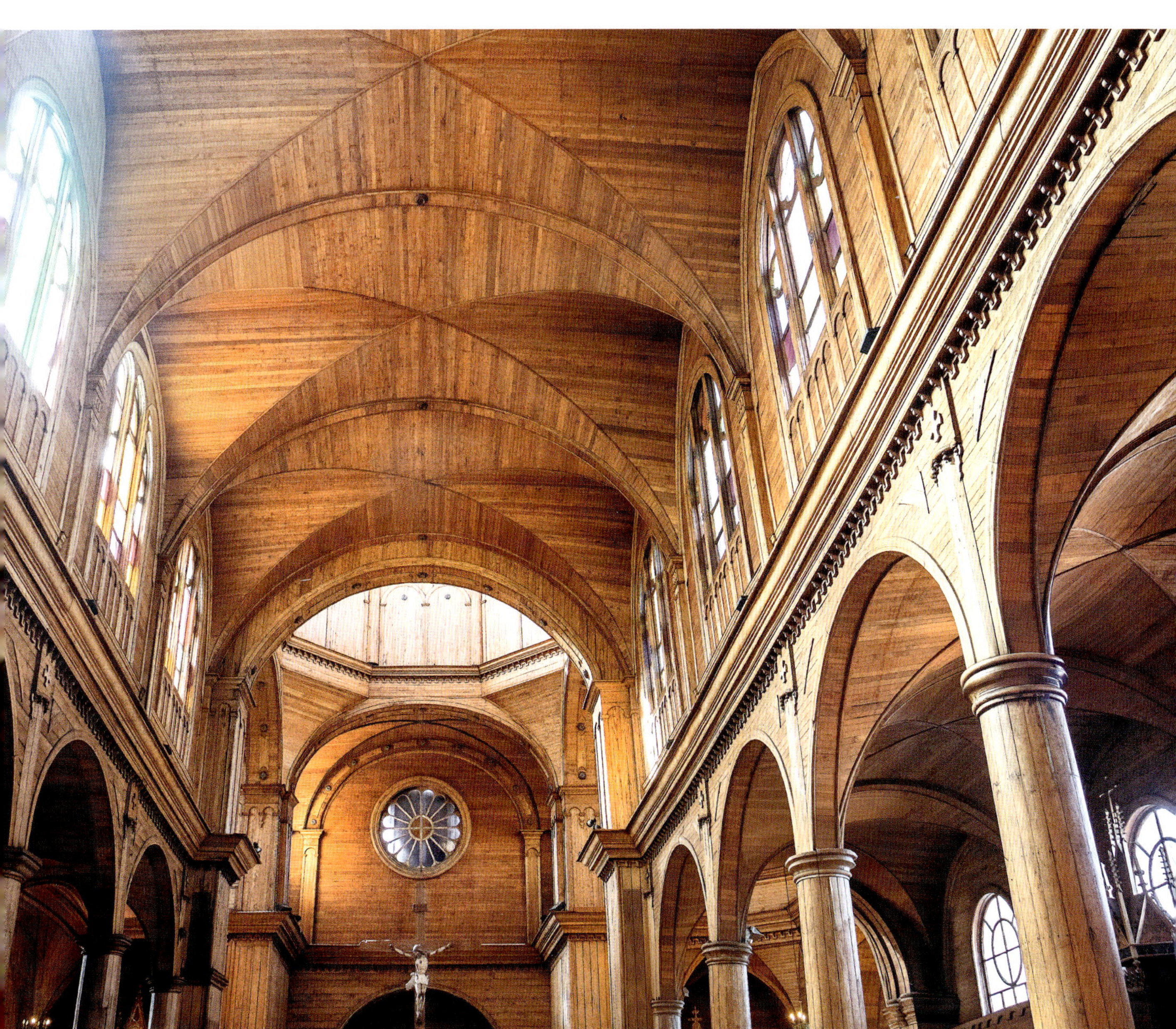

CHAPTER 9

# JURUPA OAK

*Quercus palmeri*

AGE: 13,300 YEARS

IN SEPTEMBER 2024, the Jurupa Valley City Council, in Riverside County in Southern California, approved the construction of a 917-acre area on wildlands for residential and light industrial development. On a 27-acre conical hilltop within that site, composed of steep slopes and large granite outcroppings, grows one of the oldest plants on earth: the Jurupa Oak. The distance between the visible, above-ground portion of the oak and development construction is just 450 feet.

Jurupa is a mispronunciation of the Kizh word *hurungna*, which means "place of the sagebrush." The Jurupa oak, or hurungna oak, is actually a clonal colony of *Quercus palmeri* (Palmer's oak) trees. The size of the clone and estimates of annual growth from multiple populations lead to the conclusion that the clone is more than 13,000 years old, making it one of the world's oldest living beings. The oak clone was documented by botanist Mitch Provance in the 1990s, and at the time he recognized it as growing outside the contiguous range for its species, and therefore likely an ancient clonal stand.

The isolated colony is fire dependent—it grows only after wildfires, when its burned branches are

Jurupa oaks growing among the boulders of Joshua Tree National Park.

The angular branches of a *Quercus palmeri* growing in the western Mojave Desert testify to its slow growth rate.

triggered to sprout new shoots. This oak has roughly 70 clusters of stems in a thicket that measures 82 by 26 feet (25 by 8 meters) in area and measures 3 feet (1 meter) in height.

*Quercus palmeri* is generally an evergreen shrub, or occasionally a small tree, with leathery, very spiny evergreen leaves. It grows in Baja California, Arizona, California, Nevada, New Mexico, and Utah, in dry thickets, chaparral, and mountain canyons.

Jurupa oak leaves are edged with spines, while abundant yellow catkins appear more welcoming.

About 9,000 years ago, the Kizh (pronounced "Keech") people, part of the now Gabrieleño Band of Mission Indians, arrived in the area. They, like other California tribes, consider oaks sacred. Kizh petroglyphs and grinding stones have been found in the Jurupa Hills, and it is quite possible they ground the acorns from the Jurupa oak.

The site of this Jurupa oak, as well as the surrounding area, is a designated sacred site by the

Indigenous peoples. They, and members of Friends of Jurupa Park, have requested the creation of a 100-acre Hurungna Oak Preserve.

On their website, the Friends state, "The Proposed Rio Vista Specific Plan aims to develop 406.5 acres of natural wildlands in Jurupa Valley, which entails surrounding the oldest living plant in California and the third-oldest living plant on Earth by 'light industrial' development. Under the most recent update to the proposed development, construction will take place within 450 feet (originally proposed 200 feet) of the Jurupa oak, which sits atop a small hilltop surrounded by inland sage scrub vegetation in the Jurupa Mountains. We oppose this project for a number of cultural and biological reasons, but most importantly because the oldest living organism in our state deserves to be respected and preserved in its natural context to the greatest extent possible, not surrounded by white-topped industrial-manufacturing warehouses and a business park."

A native Jurupa oak habitat, including *Quercus palmeri* east of Lake Montezuma in Yavapai County, Arizona.

CHAPTER 10

# KING'S LOMATIA

*Lomatia tasmanica*

AGE: 43,600 YEARS

THE ISLAND STATE OF TASMANIA, just 150 miles (240 kilometers) south of the Australian mainland, is an unusual place for plants. The Tasmanian temperate rainforest contains descendants of some of the most ancient of Australia's plants. Some species date back over 60 million years and were the dominant vegetation across the Australian continent long before eucalypts and acacias.

The flora of Tasmania originated in the evolutionary radiation of plant life during the Cretaceous period (145 to 66 million years ago). Tasmanian vegetation, with its 1,650 native seed-bearing plants and thousands of spore-bearing plants, ranges from alpine moorlands and heaths to temperate rainforest, eucalypt forests, and coastal heathlands.

Tasmania has three things to really boast about, botanically speaking. First is the world's tallest flowering plant and the tallest tree in the Southern Hemisphere, *Eucalyptus regnans*, the swamp gum. It can grow to 330 feet (100 meters) tall, making it the fourth-tallest tree in the world.

The colorful and charismatic blooms of king's holly, endemic to Tasmania and critically endangered.

Second is *Lomatia tasmanica*, commonly known as king's lomatia or king's holly, an unusual plant. It bears flowers, yet does not produce fruit or seed. It propagates by root suckering (rhizomes). All known existing members of *Lomatia tasmanica*, numbering just 500 stems, are found in Southwest Tasmania within a narrow corridor of land just over 0.8 miles (1.2 kilometers) in length.

Because the reproduction is vegetative, all the plants in the colony are genetically identical, making the entire grove a clone. The plant has been cloning itself for at least 43,600 years, and possibly up to 135,000 years. This makes *Lomatia tasmanica* one of the oldest living known plant clones.

It is a shrub of the family Proteaceae, and usually grows between 6 to 13 feet (2 to 4 meters) tall, has shiny green pinnate (lobed) leaves, and bears red flowers in the summer. Because it has three sets of chromosomes—33 instead of 22, a triploid—and is therefore sterile, each plant is genetically identical to its parent. Although all the plants are technically separate in that each has its own root system, they are collectively clones. Its age estimate is based on radiocarbon dating of fossilized leaf fragments; the fragments are identical to the contemporary plant in cell structure and shape, suggesting that the ancestral and modern plants are also genetically identical, fascinating to consider.

***Lomatia tasmanica*** **is in the same family as waratah, grevillea, macadamia, and protea.**

*L. tasmanica* grows in mixed forest made up of myrtle beech (*Nothophagus cunninghamii*), celery-top pine (*Phyllocladus aspleniifolius*), southern sassafras (*Atherosperma moschatum*), leatherwood (*Eucryphia lucida*), satinwood (*Nematolepis squamea*), blue-green tea tree (*Leptospermum glaucescens*), and horizontal scrub (*Anodopetalum biglandulosum*).

Charles Denison "Deny" King first recorded the plant in May 1934, while mining tin in the remote southwest of Tasmania. Winifred Curtis of the Tasmanian Herbarium named the plant in King's honor in 1967.

If a tree is defined as being a single-stemmed woody plant, then the oldest in Australia could be a huon pine (*Lagarostrobos franklinii*) in Tasmania, the oldest stem of which is up to 2,000 years old. However, huon pine is also a clone—the above-ground stems share a common root stock. If that common root stock is the base of multi-trunked tree, then that tree could be as old as 11,000 years.

Huon pine isn't actually a pine, it's a podocarp. It is a slow-growing conifer that can reach a maximum height of 98 feet (30 meters). The scalelike leaves are arranged in spirals, and the bark is light brown. It grows along riverbanks, lakeshores, and swampy locations. A stand of trees more than 10,500 years old was found in 1955 in western Tasmania, on Mount Read. Each is a genetically identical male that has reproduced vegetatively. Although no

**ABOVE** The scale-like leaves of the huon pine reveal its misnomer: it's not a pine as usually thought of in the Northern Hemisphere, but a podocarp, a conifer mainly endemic to the Southern Hemisphere.

**LEFT** A huon pine (*Lagarostrobos franklinii*) growing along the Gordon River, in Tasmania.

**ABOVE** Wollemi pine leaves, which have existed in the same formation for 60 million years.

**RIGHT** The branches of the Wollemi pine are slightly reminiscent of South America's monkey puzzle trees; indeed they are both members of the Araucariaceae family.

single tree is that age, the stand itself is identifiable as a single organism.

The oldest clonal material belonging to a tree also comes from the Southern Hemisphere. It belongs to the Wollemi pine (*Wollemia nobilis*), which may be 60 million years old. The Wollemi pine forms exact genetic copies of itself. It was thought to be extinct until a tiny remnant population in three small stands within deep canyons in Australia was discovered by David Noble, a National Parks and Wildlife Service officer, in Wollemi National Park in the Greater Blue Mountains Area in New South Wales, in 1994. The exact location is kept secret.

Once again, this is not a pine but a member of the Araucariaceae family, akin to kauri and monkey puzzle trees. It is critically endangered in the wild, but it has been successfully propagated and has been planted in many botanical gardens around the world. The Botanic Gardens of Sydney even offers homeowners tips on how to grow the tree in home gardens. From being discovered in the wild only in 1994 to having become popular in many domestic backyards is a triumph for botany.

Wollemi pine is a shade-growing, acidic-soil requiring conifer reaching up to 131 feet (40 meters) tall. It has knobbly dark brown bark and spirally arranged, flat leaves that age from lime green to yellowish green.

In Wollemi National Park, the oldest above-ground manifestation, known as the Bill Tree, is

about 400 to 450 years old. The Bill Tree's roots may be more than 1,000 years old, however. There is also substantial evidence that the tree has been cloning itself and its unique genes ever since it disappeared from the fossil record more than 60 million years ago. To determine the age of the Wollemi pine trees, a scientific team cut cross-

sections from one of the fallen trunks at the original site in Wollemi National Park and sent them to the Australian National University's forestry department for analysis. One of the most intriguing things that can't be determined due to coppicing is how old the original tree was before this particular trunk was produced. It may have been hundreds, or

**LEFT AND ABOVE** Trees in the protected original grove of the only 200 Wollemi pines remaining in Wollemi National Park, which Australian firefighters worked diligently to save during the country's devastating wildfires in 2020.

perhaps thousands of years since it was a seedling. By counting the growth rings from cross-sections of the trunk and combining this with carbon dating, the best estimate is about 350 years old. This means that the trunk started growing around the year 1650.

There are also Triassic fossil examples of the Araucariaceae family, which reached maximum diversity during the Jurassic and Cretaceous periods, between 200 and 65 million years ago, with worldwide distribution. At the end of the Cretaceous, when dinosaurs became extinct, so too did the Araucariaceae in the Northern Hemisphere. Until about the middle of the Tertiary (30 million years ago), plants in the Araucariaceae grew in the forests on supercontinent Gondwana (which included Australia, Africa, South America, Antarctica, and India). The Araucariaceae family then began a slow decline in range and diversity as flowering plants—better adapted to climate change—began to evolve and gradually displace conifers. The last fossil record of the Wollemi pine is dated at about 2 million years ago, and so the pine was thought to be extinct until its wonderful discovery just thirty years ago.

Clonal tree root systems last for millennia, as with Pando, a colony of quaking aspens (*Populus tremuloides*) in Utah covered earlier in this volume, that has been estimated to be as old as 80,000 years. For longevity, send in the clones.

The female cones of the Wollemi pine.

CHAPTER 11

# LOSH RUN BOX HUCKLEBERRY

*Gaylussacia brachycera*

AGE: 1,300 TO 8,000 YEARS

BOX HUCKLEBERRY MAY BE DIMINUTIVE, but no one can argue that it deserves respect.

*Gaylussacia brachycera*, commonly known as box huckleberry or box-leaved whortleberry, is a North American shrub in the blueberry family, Ericaceae. It is native to the east-central United States, including Pennsylvania, Delaware, Maryland, Virginia, West Virginia, North Carolina, Kentucky, and Tennessee. It has evergreen boxwood-like leaves, and has white urn-shaped flowers in the early summer that develop to become blue, edible berries in late summer. It grows just to about 1 foot (0.3 meters) high.

There are two colonies of box huckleberry of note, and both are in Pennsylvania. One, in Losh Run,is estimated to be as old as 8,000 years; the other, the Hoverter and Sholl box huckleberry, is estimated to be between 1,000 and 1,400 years old.

The Losh Run huckleberry was first discovered in 1920 by Harvey Ward. Using the growth rate of the

**LEFT** Box huckleberry, a clonal plant generally estimated to be at least 1,300 years old.

**FOLLOWING PAGES** The inflorescence of box huckleberry, still producing abundant fruit after thousands of years.

rhizomes and the size of the colony, subsequent botanists estimated the age of the Losh Run colony to be around 13,000 years, although that has been revised down to 8,000 years. Still, impressive.

Most of the Losh Run colony was unfortunately destroyed due to road construction. Today, only fragments of the original plant survive, scattered across private properties.

The Hoverter and Sholl box huckleberry is protected within an eponymous natural area in the Tuscarora State Forest, near New Bloomfield. A 0.25-mile (0.40-kilometer) path loops around the site. While the plants' height is not impressive, its width is—it easily stretches for hundreds of feet in all directions.

Surrounding the box huckleberry is a forest of native plants with trees such as white pine (*Pinus strobus*), eastern hemlock (*Tsuga canadensis*), and black, red, and white oak (*Quercus velutina, Quercus rubra,* and *Quercus alba*). Wildflowers are prolific. There are colonies of pink lady's slipper (*Cypripedium acaule*), white trillium (*Trillium grandiflorum*), masses of hay-scented fern (*Dennstaedtia punctilobula*), and Christmas fern (*Polystichum acrostichoides*), too.

The Hoverter and Sholl conservation area, near New Bloomfield, Pennsylvania, is designated a National Natural Landmark due to the huckleberry's uniqueness, though it only covers ten acres.

HOVERTER AND SHOLL
BOX
HUCKLEBERRY
NATURAL
AREA
TUSCARORA
STATE FOREST
DEPARTMENT OF
CONSERVATION & NATURAL RESOURCES

CHAPTER 12

# MONGARLOWE MALLEE

*Eucalyptus recurva*
AGE: 3,000 TO 13,000 YEARS

THE ICE AGE GUM, or Mongarlowe mallee, is the rarest eucalyptus. Only five plants are recorded to be alive, and they are in two separate locations spread over an 18.6-mile (30 kilometer) range in the southern tablelands of New South Wales, 139 miles (224 kilometers) southwest of Sydney, Australia. The range is so large, and the individuals so far apart from each other—at least 1¼ miles (2 kilometers) —that natural pollination doesn't happen. Without human assistance, they are fated to become extinct.

The specimens are in a location rightly kept secret, close to Mongarlowe, a village of about 117 people. One tree is 3,000 years old, with others possibly about 13,000 years old. This is where *Eucalyptus recurva* gets its common name, ice age gum, as the plant is believed to have survived since the last Ice Age, 25,000 to 11,700 years ago.

The geology and climate of the region gives partial insight into the species's longevity: the formation of the Southern Tablelands is attributed to the uplift of the Great Dividing Range, which caused the

The locations of the five living Mongarlowe mallee plants known to exist are kept secret by the New South Wales government; they grow in a mallee environment similar to this, famous for multi-branched trees.

**ABOVE** A close-up of this rare eucalyptus's backward-curving leaves.

**RIGHT** The Mongarlowe mallee's most distinguishing habit is its multistemmed branches that grow directly up from an underground lignotuber.

erosion of the surrounding areas and the deposit of alluvial sediments in the region. The land is high and flat, and has been largely cleared for grazing. It is a temperate grassland with soils made up of loamy red clay soil of moderate-to-low fertility and areas of sandstone and shale. Around the Golden Triangle, near Atherton, it's fertile red soil. Annual rainfall in this diverse region varies from 19.6 to 4.7 inches (500 mm to 1,200 mm) and frost-free periods vary from 140 to 260 days a year, depending on altitude. The trees' survival is helped in part due to the fact that they grow on uncultivated heathland of shallow sandy loam on quartzite slopes that sheep and cattle avoid.

*Mallee* is the Wemba Wemba language's term for trees and shrubs growing near water, mainly in the eucalyptus family. Mallee are distinguished by having multiple stems growing from an underground lignotuber—a subterranean woody organ. It is the lignotuber that survives after fire and other trauma and sprouts new growth afterward. The largest Mongarlowe mallee has a lignotuber base 39 feet (12 meters) across, sprouting with multiple trunks. It is estimated to be 13,000 years old, with a growth rate of 0.07 inches (2 millimeters) a year.

*Eucalyptus recurva* was only recorded by botanists in the late 1980s. It is a small mallee

generally growing to a maximum height of around 5 feet (1.5 meters). It has multicolored bark of orange, green, or yellow that sheds in long ribbons. The backward-curving leaves are arranged in opposite pairs and are elliptical or egg-shaped and are pale underneath. White flowers appear for a brief time in January.

Associated heathland plants are the dominant dwarf she-oak (*Allocasuarina nana*), growing to a height of 6.7 inches (2 meters) with erect, whorled scalelike leaves, and with barrel-shaped cones, and finger hakea (*Hakea dactyloides*). This species of hakea is so called because of its digit-like leaves. Small white flowers appear in early summer.

With only five known plants in existence, the *Eucalyptus recurva* is in great danger of extinction. The remaining plants are closely protected by the Australian government, and attempts have been made to cross-pollinate the existing plants to produce viable offspring. The New South Wales National Parks and Wildlife Service has outlined an extensive plan for conserving and propagating the Mongarlowe mallee plants. Let us hope their efforts are fruitful.

The *Eucalyptus recurva* grows only in heathland, a critically endangered type of environment.

CHAPTER 13

# OLD TJIKKO

*Picea abies*

AGE: 9,550 YEARS

OLD TJIKKO IS a charismatic, but ragged, tree—what you might expect from anyone who's reached the age of 600 years. Its root system, to boot, has reached a magnificent 9,550 years. Above ground, it looks like an unassuming 16-foot-tall (4.87 meters) Norwegian spruce (*Picea abies*). It grows high atop the hard sandstone plateau of Fulufjellet Mountain, divided between Sweden and Norway, with Old Tjikko's trunk growing on the Swedish side. The sedimentary sandstone on which the tree grows is Trysil sandstone, which has a deep reddish color. It was deposited there 1.4 billion years ago. The soil is rich in quartz, is acidic, and is nutrient-poor. The harsh climate and thin soil have contributed to the tree's longevity, as the cold climate slows down the growth—and aging—process.

Old Tjikko was discovered by Leif Kullman, a professor emeritus of physical geography at Umeå University, in 2004. He named the tree after his late dog, Tjikko.

For many years the spruce tree has been regarded as a relative newcomer among the Swedish mountain region's species. "Our results have shown the

This tree has been surviving on a harsh sandstone mountaintop, cloning itself repeatedly, for almost 10,000 years.

**ABOVE** Although the *Picea abies* produces cones, it can also reproduce itself clonally.

**RIGHT** A stand of *Picea abies* shows how they look when they grow in a grove, rather than as a solitary specimen like Old Tjikko.

complete opposite, that the spruce is one of the oldest known trees in the mountain range," Kullman says. A fascinating discovery was made under the crown of a spruce in Fulu Mountain, in Dalarna. Scientists found four "generations" of spruce remains in the form of cones and wood produced from the highest grounds. The discovery showed trees of 375, 5,660, 9,000, and 9,550 years old, and everything displayed clear signs that they had the same genetic makeup as the trees above them.

Since spruce trees can procreate with root-penetrating branches, they can produce exact copies, or clones. The tree now growing above the finding place and the wood pieces dating to 9,550 years ago have the same genetic material.

Previously, pine trees in North America had been cited as the oldest, at 4,000 to 5,000 years old. In the Swedish mountains, from Lapland in the North to Dalarna in the South, scientists have found a cluster of around twenty spruces that are over 8,000 years old. Although summers have been colder over the past 10,000 years, these trees have

survived harsh weather conditions due to their ability to push out a new trunk as the other one dies. "The average increase in temperature during the summers over the past hundred years has risen one degree in the mountain areas," Kullman says.

Therefore, we can now see that these spruces have begun to straighten themselves out. There is also evidence that spruces are the species that can best give us insight into climate change: their ability to survive harsh conditions presents plenty of questions and challenges for researchers. Have the spruces that migrated here during the Ice Age as seeds from the east—621 miles (1,000 kilometers) over the inland ice—covered Scandinavia?

"My research indicates that spruces have spent winters in places west or southwest of Norway, where the climate was not as harsh, in order to later quickly spread northerly along the ice-free coastal strip," explains Kullman. "In some way, they have also successfully found their way to the Swedish mountains."

Younger branches grow radially around the base of Old Tjikko, an adaptation likely due to the harsh conditions.

CHAPTER 14

# OLIVE

*Olea europaea*
AGE: 300 YEARS

IMAGINE THREE HUNDRED YEARS AGO. A human or other animal consumes the salty, fleshy fruit of an olive, then discards its pit (pyrena). It lays in the soil for almost three months, produces a root, then two seed leaves. A tree is born.

It grows rapidly in the stony calcareous soil and bright sunlight of the Mediterranean; silvery evergreen leaves emerge on a green stem. The stem becomes thicker, woodier, turns into a proper trunk. After six or ten years, the tree matures enough to produce flowers, which turn later in the season into one of the most desired fruits in the world: olives

Few fruits have perhaps proved so important to Western civilization as the olive. The first wild olive (oleaster) wood (*Olea europaea*) found being used in conjunction with human activity, as fuel in a firepit, is in Klissoura Cave in southern Greece, which is dated to 61,140–55,230 BCE. It was also found at Higueral de Valleja, Cadiz, Spain, which dates to 42,630–41,390 BCE.

These fecund trees have of course been cultivated in orchards for many centuries (some estimate for up to 7,000 or 8,000 years, even), since the olives provided food, oil for perfume, ritual use, and trade. Residues found on the interiors of pots are evidence

A very old olive tree growing in front of the Pont du Gard aqueduct, in southern France.

of the earliest domestic use of the olive. In one cave in Crete, archaeologists revealed that Cretans were using olive oil in their cooking as early as 6,000 years ago.

Fossil pollen evidence tells us that the southern Levant—the area loosely covered by modern-day Israel, Palestine, and Jordan, southern Lebanon, southern Syria, and the borderlands between Syria and Turkey—were areas of primary olive cultivation as early as 6,500 years BCE, and early/mid-sixth millennium BCE cultivation occurred in the Aegean (on the island of Crete).

The growing and management of olive trees on a comparatively large scale was an economically revolutionary advancement for early Mediterranean villages, and enhanced agricultural, economic, and social prosperity. Southern Levant and Aegean olive cultivation then spread across the Mediterranean. In Anatolia, large-scale olive horticulture has been recorded by 3,200 BCE, in mainland Italy by 3,400 BCE, and in the Iberian Peninsula by the mid/late third millennium BCE. The Roman Empire undertook vast plantings of olive groves. Large estates were established around these, and one, described by Cato, had an annual yield of 100,000 liters of oil. The Romans were responsible for bringing about a significant increase in olive oil production beginning between 200 BCE and 200 CE. Olive oil production became semi-industrialized at sites such as Hendek Kale in Turkey, Byzacena in Tunisia, and Tripolitania, in Libya, where 750 separate olive oil production sites have been documented.

**LEFT** A floral collar found in Tutankhamun's embalming cache (c. 1336–1327 BCE), which includes olive leaves, cornflowers, nightshade berries, and poppies.

**RIGHT** An amphora from the Panathenaic games (c. 510 BCE), which was filled with 40 liters of olive oil harvested from the sacred groves of Athena and awarded as a prize.

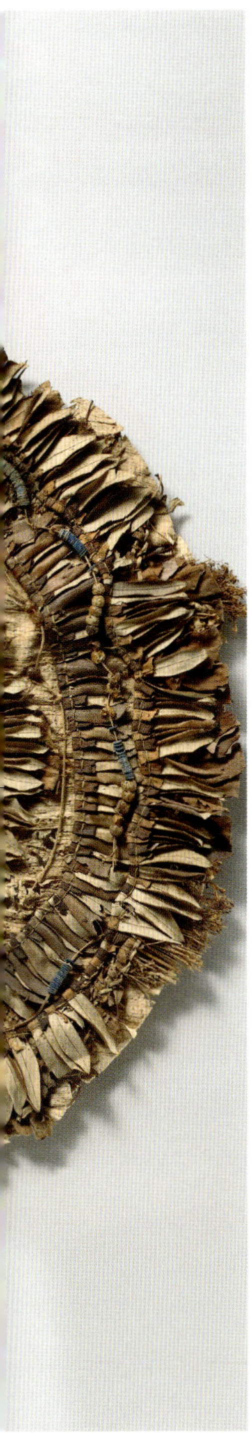

Estimates of oil production during the Roman Era are of up to 8 million gallons (30 million liters) per year was produced in Tripolitania, and up to 10.5 million gallons (40 million liters) in Byzacena.

More proof of olive oil production comes from numerous installations discovered in various excavations in Crete. Deep, large-scale clay tubs containing liquid were found there, along with mortars and basins suitable for crushing fruit. By the late Minoan Era (1400–1100 BCE), massive stone-spouted press-beds, resting on stone platforms, were used. The Heraklion Archaeological Museum has an impressive collection of olive jars and a display of olive-oil-processing technology from the that period.

Olive oil was used in the ancient Mediterranean in a variety of ways beyond cooking. It was also a base for cosmetics and beauty products. Perfume had long been used in Ancient Egypt and, with the advent of olive oil production on a substantial scale, perfumers in the Levant and the Aegean began to mix green olive oil with various herbs, spices, and flowers. Henna perfume was a mixture of henna (*Lawsonia inermis*), green olive oil, sweet flag, myrrh, cardamom, southernwood, and all-heal. One of the first-known popular cosmetics was created by Galen (129–216 CE), a Greek physician who

The Temple of Concordia in Valley of the Temples, Agrigento, Sicily, Italy, is surrounded by ancient olive groves.

mixed olive oil, beeswax, and rose water to form a face cream.

It was later that olive oil began to be used as fuel in lamps; these did not appear in Ancient Greece until the seventh century BCE. These were shallow clay cups filled with olive oil, with a wick emanating from a small spout. Olive oil—along with tallow, beeswax, fish oil, and whale oil—were used in lamps and lanterns until the late eighteenth century, when kerosene was developed.

The medicinal properties of olive oil were highly valued by ancient doctors. The Roman Emperor Julian's personal physician used olive oil as a base for antiseptic plasters and ointments to soothe pain and heal wounds, cuts, and burns, following the recommendations of the famous Greek doctor Hippocrates. In the Middle East still today, many believe that drinking half a cup of olive oil before breakfast will "clear the system." Some people even maintain that olive oil is a powerful aphrodisiac, and an old Greek custom is to give newlyweds bread dipped in olive oil to encourage conception. And these ancient medics were correct: dried olives contain 51.90% fat, 30.07% water, 10.45% carbohydrates, 5.24% protein, and 2.33% mineral matter, and are exceptionally rich in potassium. Olive oil is rich in monounsaturated fat, and can reduce the LDL (bad) cholesterol without reducing

One of the oldest forms of extracting olive oil was to use a stone press, as with this antique Roman version.

the HDL (good) cholesterol in the blood. Olives are also particularly rich in antioxidants, including oleuropein, hydroxytyrsol and quercetin. Observational studies suggest that a diet high in olives may also protect against osteoporosis.

Greek mythology is abundant with legends and mentions of olive trees. Perhaps the most notable is the one which explains how the olive tree was first created and how Athens got its name. Both Athena, goddess of wisdom, and Poseidon, god of the sea, volunteered to become protector over a newly built city. The city's king, Cecrops, suggested they both enter a contest to decide who would get the honor. Each had to offer the city a gift. The city would then be named after the god or goddess whose gift was judged by the citizens as the most precious, useful, and divine. Poseidon raised his trident and struck a rock, creating a spring of salty water which symbolized his gift of maritime prowess. Athena struck a rock with her spear and produced the olive tree, an offering signifying fruitfulness and peace. The citizens chose Athena's, and she was declared the patroness of the city now named after her.

Aristaeus, the son of Apollo and Cyrene, was credited with developing and perfecting many rural arts, including how to tame and cultivate the wild oleaster in order to make it bear olives and how to process the fruits into olive oil.

In Greek myth, Athena gifted an olive tree to Cecrops, the first king of the major city—he considered it such a valuable present that he named Athens after her.

The olive tree was also an important cultural and religious symbol for the Roman Empire. Legend has it that the heroic founders of Rome, brothers Romulus and Remus, were born in the shade of an olive tree—before being nurtured by a she-wolf.

In Roman mythology, the goddess of wisdom, Minerva, is credited with creating the first olive tree, in a legend that echoes the Greek story. The legend tells of a gift-giving competition between Minerva and the god of oceans, Neptune. Neptune gave the people a spring of salty water while Minerva presented them with an olive tree. The people gratefully accepted the olive tree as a source of food, medicine, and wood.

The olive branch is touted as a symbol of peace by the goddess Pax (Eirene in Greek mythology) and the god Mars the Pacifier, both appearing on Roman Imperial coins. In periods of war, rulers would send couriers with a symbolic olive branch in their hands to announce peace or to call for a truce with their enemies. Oil and the olive tree are also often cited in *The Iliad* and *The Odyssey*. Ulysses's bed was carved from a large olive tree, and his body was covered in and washed with oil regularly to maintain his strength and youth.

The dead used to be placed on a bed of olive leaves and covered in oil, and tombs were adorned

Arbequina olive branches with ripening fruit.

with olive wreaths and branches. At the games played in honor of Zeus in Olympia, athletes were rewarded with amphoras of oil, and winners were crowned with an olive wreath. It was common practice among athletes, who competed naked, to massage their bodies with oil. Oiling one's body and hair was a regular practice also among common people, who used olive oil infused with herbs and flower essences.

The Bible also tells the story of the dove that returned to Noah's ark carrying an olive branch, a symbol of the restored peace between God and mankind. Jesus descended from the Mount of Olives to enter Jerusalem, and Gethsemane, where he was arrested, means "olive press."

Olives and olive oil are also mentioned in the Qur'an six times in six verses: "Allah is the Light of the heavens and the earth. The example of His light is like a niche within which is a lamp, the lamp is within glass, the glass as if it were a pearly star lit from the oil of the blessed olive tree."

The symbolism has endured into the modern era as well, notably on the Great Seal of the United States, designed in 1776. It features a bald eagle grasping an olive branch in its right talon. The United Nations flag also features olive branches to signify its commitment to peacekeeping.

Ancient olive trees in the Garden of Gethsemane.

At the coronation of King Charles III in May 2023, he was anointed with chrism oil, a mixture of olive oil harvested from two groves on the Mount of Olives, and sesame oil, rose, jasmine, cinnamon, neroli, amber, and orange blossom.

Let's return to the seedling olive tree that opened this chapter. After 300 years, it's become enormous. Olive trees are also remarked for generally looking much older than they are. This one might have a trunk is 30 feet (10 meters) in circumference at its base, and could stand 15 feet (4.5 meters high). Its girth and its height are not just due to its age but also to centuries of annual pruning. The trunk twists and turns, giving it a gnarled appearance we associate with great age. The huge trunk, however, is hollow; the heartwood of olives rots from fungi, while the sapwood remains intact, sustaining the tree.

There are many examples of "ancient" olive trees throughout the Mediterranean. Various villages claim to have 3,000-to-5,000-year-old trees. Many of the most famous trees have even been fenced off and adorned with plaques making a claim of age.

In the village of Ano Vouves, Crete, a famous tree visited by thousands of tourists is reputed to be 3,500 to 5,000 years old. The tree does remain productive to this day, having been grafted with the cultivar 'Tsounati'.

Simliarly, a grove composed of sixteen olive trees in Bchaaleh, Lebanon, is known as "the sisters." Local folklore says they are about 6,000 years old.

Ancient olive trees are appreciated for their gnarled bark's aesthetic addition to gardens.

An ancient olive tree known as Oliveira de Mouchão, in Mouriscas, Portugal, is currently one of the oldest living olive trees in the world, or so states social media. It is indeed exceptionally tall and wide, measuring 25 feet (7.80 meters) in height, and at ground level, is 36 feet (11.20 meters) in girth.

Tourists flock to see these ancient trees, and locals with a vested interest in encouraging tourism extol their age and ability to still produce fruit. But are they as old as is claimed? For an answer to that, we must turn to science.

In dendrochronology, core samples are often used to extract a record of tree rings, and generally each ring marks the passage of one year in the life of the tree. The rings, however, are more visible in trees that grow in temperate zones, where the seasons differ markedly. A second dating method, radiocarbon dating, determines the age of an object containing organic material by assessing levels of carbon-14 in wood.

Direct reading of tree ring chronologies is a complex science, for several reasons. First, contrary to the single-ring-per-year pattern, alternating poor and favorable conditions, such as midsummer droughts, can result in several rings forming each year. In addition, particular tree species often present what specialists call "missing rings." Missing rings are rare in hardwoods such as oak, elm, and redwoods, but quite common in olives.

Radiocarbon dating is accurate as an overall science, but since the inner and oldest part of the trunk in olive trees usually rots away as the tree ages, it excludes accurate radiocarbon analysis of

An olive in the village of Ano Vouves, on the island of Crete, touted to be between 3,500 and 5,000 years old.

material from the first years of a tree's life. To complicate things more, olives often branch internally over different periods, and in turn those branches merge and become part of what we see as the trunk, mingling timelines. Most radiocarbon dating of internal wood from living olive trees has shown that olive trees are rarely older than 300 years.

At best, the idea that any living olive tree could be thousands of years old is a romantic fabrication. It pleases us to think that a tree we see growing before us produced olives enjoyed by the earliest ancient inhabitants of Europe and the Levant, or perhaps even having been visited by historical figures as grand as Roman emperors, or, as in the case of the Garden of Gethsemane, Jesus himself. We poetically imagine rough-handed farmers and their families picking olives, rustically pressing fresh olive oil, filling up amphora, and loading them on to Greek ships to be traded all across the coastline of the Mediterranean.

We imagine the trees growing stoically, impervious to the human dramas like wars, politics, and shifting borders happening around them. We like to imagine them continuing to grow long past the end of our own lifetimes, and fantasize that perhaps our children's children might press their hands to the same trunk we once caressed.

For the poetic, it does not matter that none of this can be true. The trees may not be as old as they're often claimed to be, but they can still be celebrated as a species with an uncanny ability to make us all stop and think about history. Their long entanglement with our own species helps us see them as markers of what their singular fruit has helped us achieve as a civilization.

These trees in Lebanon are reportedly 6,000 years old—likely local legend.

CHAPTER 15

# PIPAL

*Ficus religiosa*
AGE: 100 YEARS+

ONE OF THE MOST IMPORTANT STORIES in Buddhist mythology is about a strikingly large tree. According to the story, Gautama achieved enlightenment while sitting under a pipal tree, a *Ficus religiosa*.

According to tradition, the Buddha who lived in the fifth century BCE was born in Lumbini, in what is now Nepal. He was the son of a local ruler, and spent much of his life in what is now India. Some records documenting the life of the Buddha exist in texts on monastic discipline, but more are found in the suttas, the discourses of the Buddha. The suttas were originally transmitted orally, by communal chanting, then written down centuries later.

Embellished features were added to the story, giving us the myths we have today. But what about fig trees, then as well as now, continues to stimulate the human imagination?

There are actually 877 species in the genus *Ficus* —a mix of pantropical trees, shrubs, vines, and epiphytes. These in turn all belong to the mulberry family, Moraceae. The largest tree in the world is a fig, a *Ficus benghalensis* that grows near Kolkata, India and occupies about 4.67 acres (18,918 square

A pipal grows through the charismatic ruins of Angkor Archaeological Park in Siem Reap, Cambodia.

meters, 1.89 hectares). On the other extreme, the smallest fig fruit is likely that of the *Ficus excavata*, an epiphyte growing high in the canopy of diptero-carps in Borneo; its figs are as small as 0.1 inches (3 millimeters) in diameter. One of the tastiest fruits in the world, and one of the first fruits to be cultivated by humans, is the fig from *Ficus carica*, native to the Mediterranean and western and southern Asia.

But back to the Buddha. As the story goes, Gautama sat beneath a pipal tree and began to meditate. According to some traditions, he realized enlightenment in one night. Others say it took three days and three nights, while others say forty-five days. Mara, the lord of death, wished to stop Siddhartha's quest for enlightenment, so he brought his most beautiful daughters to Bodh Gaya to seduce him. But Siddhartha did not move. Then Mara sent armies of demons to attack him. Siddhartha sat still and untouched, sheltered.

Then Siddhartha reached out his right hand to touch the earth, and the earth itself spoke: "I bear you witness!" To this day, the Buddha often is portrayed in this "earth witness" posture, with his left hand, palm upright, in his lap, and his right hand touching the earth. Eventually, he formulated the Four Noble Truths and the Eightfold Path to help people find the way to enlightenment. He then left Bodh Gaya and went out to teach.

The story is ancient, but the tree that currently grows at the site where this extraordinary event took place is not.

In 1862, the British archaeologist Sir Alexander Cunningham wrote about the site as the first entry in the first volume of his *Archaeological Survey of India*:

> "Buddha-Gaya is famous as the locality of the holy Pipal tree under which Sakya Sinha sat for

A *Ficus religiosa* will fruit year-round in its native habitat, with figs growing directly from the trunk and branches.

six years in mental abstraction, until he obtained Buddhahood. The name is usually written Buddha-Gaya; but as it is commonly pronounced Bodh-Gaya, I have little doubt that it was originally called Bodhi-Gaya, after the celebrated Bodhi-drum or 'tree of knowledge.' A celebrated Bodhi tree still grows at this site, but is very much decayed; one large stem, with three branches to the westward, is still green, but the other branches are barkless and rotten.

The green branch might even belong to some younger tree, as there are numerous stems of apparently different trees clustered together. The tree must have been renewed frequently, as the present Pipal is standing on a terrace at least 30 feet above the level of the surrounding country. It was in full vigour in 1811, when seen by Dr. Buchanan who describes it as in all probability not exceeding 100 years of age."

However, the tree decayed further and, in 1876, the remaining tree was destroyed in a storm. In 1881, Cunningham planted a new Bodhi tree on the same site. There is therefore considerable doubt as to whether the present tree at Bodh Gaya is even a scion of the original Bodhi tree.

According to the *Mahavamsa*, the chronicle of the Sinhalese, the Sri Maha Bodhi in Sri Lanka was planted in 288 BCE. "In this year (the twelfth year of King Ashoka's reign) the right branch (a sapling) of the Bodhi tree was brought by Sanghamittā (a Buddhist nun) to Anurādhapura and planted."

It has been growing for over 2,300 years and is listed as the oldest living human-planted tree in the world with a known planting date.

**ABOVE** A statue of the Buddha with the roots of a pipal growing around it in Ayutthaya, Thailand.

**LEFT** Monks meditating under the Ananda Bodhi Tree, an offshoot of the tree under which Gautama Buddha is said to have attained enlightenment.

**ABOVE** Devout Buddhists place support sticks beneath a pipal at Wat Chang Kham Temple in Chiang Rai, Thailand.

**RIGHT** A shrine beneath a *Ficus religiosa* tree in Kandy, in the central province of Sri Lanka.

The two ways of scientifically verifying the age of a tree are usually by tree rings and carbon dating, and there is not a single reference to the carbon dating of the Sri Maha Bodhi. So, we are left with written records—the *Mahavamsa*—written in the style of an epic poem. It chronicles the history of Sri Lanka from the epoch of Theravada Buddhism (1765 BCE) to King Mahasena (948–921 BCE). It was first composed in the fifth century CE. This lapse in time from event to record must lead to doubt as to the age of the Sri Maha Bodhi, and it is possible that claims of great age for the tree is a form of arboricultural nationalism, symbolizing the august history of the Sinhalese.

The Foster Botanical Garden in Honolulu, Hawaii, has a clone of the bodhi tree that was planted in 1913. A sapling of the Maha bodhi tree was in Chennai, India, in year 1950. And at the Theosophical Society, in Thousand Oaks, California, there is a young sapling scion in a nearby park. Another young scion was planted in April 2008 at Kurilpa Point, the site of the Queensland Art Gallery and Gallery of Modern Art, by the artist Lee Mingwei, as the centerpiece to his Bhodi Tree Project, which is described as a living artwork.

*Ficus religiosa* is much more than a symbol of the sacred, though it may not be a coincidence that humans first ascribed it a certain power after recognizing its medicinal value. These are only just being studied scientifically, but we know the pipal's bioactive compounds have been used in many types of pharmacology, traditional as well as modern. The bark of the tree contains antibacterial compounds.

Phytochemicals in the fruit have been reported to have medicinal properties that are antibacterial, antidiabetic, and anticonvulsant. The leaf juices are used to treat vomiting, asthma, cough, and diarrhea. Scientists are in the process of determining the effectiveness of its extracts in anticancer activity, particularly for breast and cervical cancers.

There is no doubt that the history of the Bodhi tree itself, however, is one faith, not science, though it's remarkable that trees can be so central to a religion with over 320 million modern practitioners.

*Thus with a hundred roots the great Bodhi-tree set itself there in the fragrant earth, converting the people to the faith. Ten cubits long was the stem; five lovely branches (were thereon), each four cubits long and (each) adorned with five fruits, and on these branches were a thousand twigs. Such was the ravishing and auspicious great Bodhi-tree.*

*At the moment that the great Bodhi-tree set itself in the vase the earth quaked and wonders of many kinds came to pass. By the resounding of the instruments of music (which gave out sound) of themselves among gods and men, by the ringing-out of the shout of salutation from the hosts of devas and brahmas, by the crash of the clouds, (the voices) of beasts and birds, of the yakkhas and so forth and by the crash of the quaking of the earth all was in one tumult.*

*Beautiful rays of six colours going forth from the fruits and leaves of the Bodhi-tree made the whole universe to shine.*

—"The Receiving of the Great Bodhi-Tree."
*The Mahavamsa*

The *Ficus benghalensis* is famous for its aerial roots; this one grows near Mendut Temple in Java, Indonesia.

CHAPTER 16

# PLANTS IN STONE: THE FOSSILS

AGE: 4 MILLION YEARS+

WHILE THIS BOOK IS ABOUT PLANTS alive today, it's worth taking a detour into what we can learn about them and their long-lived adaptations from their predecessors, known only to us as fossils. It seems that every month, we find new evidence of plant fossils dating farther back in Earth's history than we expected. Paleobotanists and geoscientists have been remarkably busy.

Recently, fossilized trees dating back 390 million years were found in England. They are roughly 4 million years older than the previous record holder, cladoxylopsid trees found in New York's Gilboa Fossil Forest.

These newest fossilized specimens were found in the sandstone cliffs along the Devon and Somerset coast. Known as Calamophyton, they look like relatives of today's palm trees. Their trunks were thin and hollow in the center, and they stood between 6.5 and 13 feet (2 and 4 meters ) tall. They

Charles R. Knight's mural representing what early land plants in the Devonian region might have looked like in the Paleozoic Era, 320 million years ago.

**ABOVE** A drawing of Calamophyton trees based on fossils found in Devon and Somerset, United Kingdom, dating to 390 million years ago.

did not have leaves; their branches were covered in twig-like structures.

The Calamophyton forest dates to the Devonian period, between 358 million and 419 million years ago. During the Devonian period, the north Devon and west Somerset coasts were not attached to the rest of England, but were connected to parts of Germany and Belgium, where similar Devonian fossils have since been found.

The cladoxylopsid trees found in New York had a central trunk topped by several lateral branches. Fossils of these plants originate in the Middle Devonian to Early Carboniferous periods (390 to 320 million years ago).

Fossils of the very earliest plants to have colonized land were found in Argentina. They are liverworts, Marchantiophyta, simple plants without stems or roots. Liverworts are probably the ancestors of all land plants. The discovery puts back by 10 million years the colonization of land by plants and suggests that a diversity of land plants had evolved by 472 million years ago.

This discovery was made by a team of researchers led by Claudia Rubinstein of the department of palaeontology at the Argentine Institute of Snow, Ice and Environmental Research. Samples of sediment were collected from the Rio Capillas, in the Sierras Subandinas in the Central Andean Basin of northwest Argentina. In the sediment, the team found hardy fossilized spores, cryptospores, dating from between 473 and 471 million years ago.

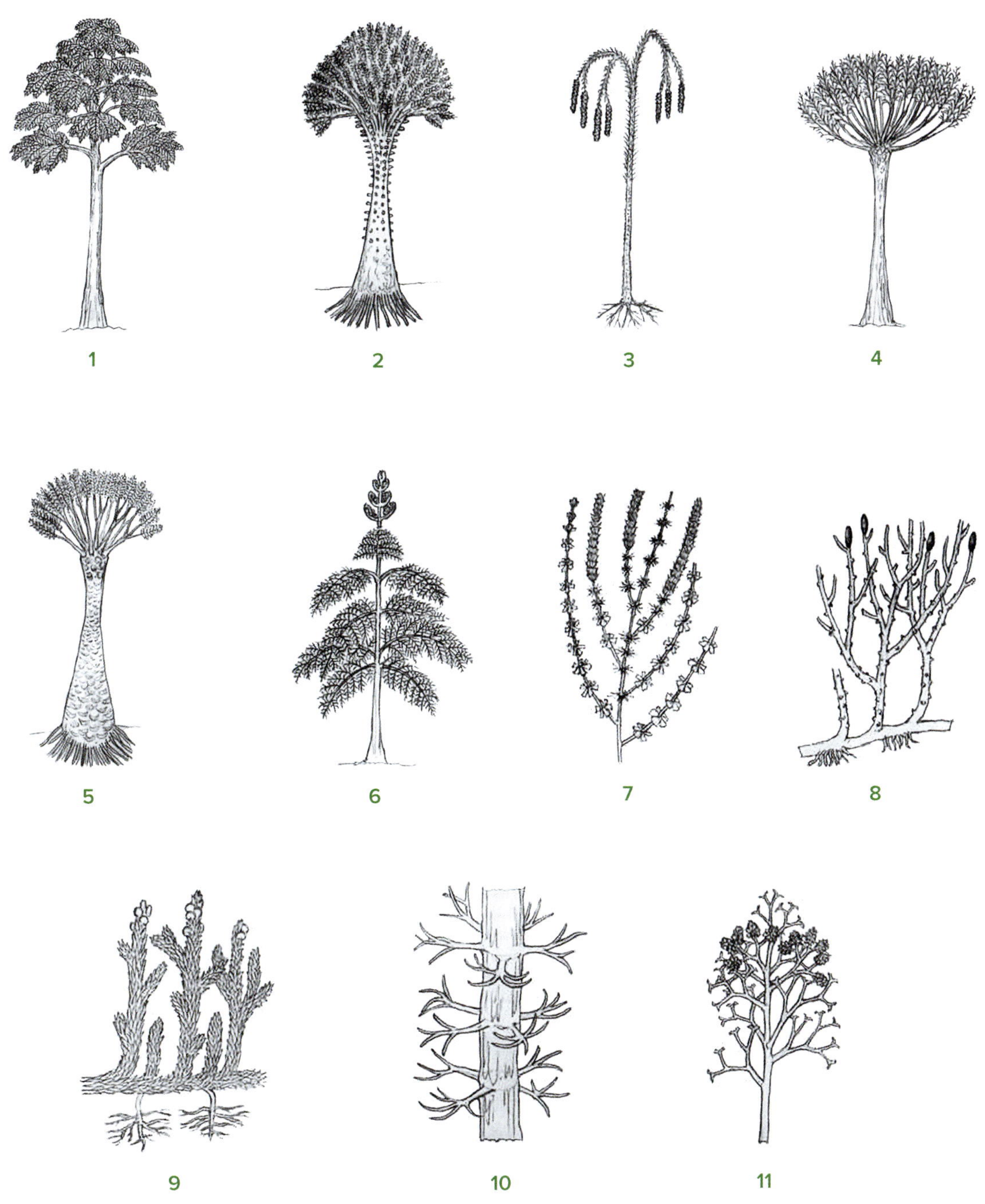


Drawings from fossils of trees found among the Devonian deposit: 1. *Archaeopteris macilenta* 2. *Calamophyton primaevum* 3. *Guangdedendron micrum* 4. *Pseudosporochnus nodosus* 5. *Wattiezagivetiana* 6. *Tetraxylopteris reposana* 7. *Sphenophyllum lungtanense* 8. *Rhynia gwynne-vaughanii* 9. *Asteroxylon mackiei* 10. *Estinnophyton yunnanense* 11. *Psilophyton dawsonii.*

Fossils from the Devonian deposit: 1. *Archaepteris*. 2 and 3: *Floragerminis*. 4. *Floragerminis jurassica*. 5. *Calamophyton*.

The researchers' best estimate is that plant colonization of land could have occurred during the early Ordovician period (488 to 472 million years ago), or even during the late Cambrian period (499 to 488 million years ago).

In China, researchers have uncovered the earliest example of a flower bud—a 164-million-year-old plant fossil. That discovery pushes back the emergence of flowering plants into the Jurassic period, between 145 and 201 million years ago. The fossil was uncovered in the Inner Mongolia region and contains a stem, a leafy branch, a bulbous fruit, and a tiny flower bud. The researchers have named the new species *Florigerminis jurassica*.

Drilling cores from Switzerland have revealed the oldest known fossils of the direct ancestors of flowering plants: 240-million-year-old pollen grains. These are evidence that flowering plants evolved 100 million years earlier than previously thought. An uninterrupted sequence of fossilized pollen from flowers begins in the Early Cretaceous, approximately 140 million years ago, and it is assumed that flowering plants first evolved around that time. But the study in Switzerland implies that flowering plants may have originated in the Early Triassic (between 252 to 247 million years ago).

The findings keep coming. The earliest known fossil of a terrestrial plant's entire structure is *Cooksonia barrandei*, which flourished 432 million

**TOP** A Gilboa Dam fossilized Wattieza tree stump, from Newtown Creek Nature Walk in Brooklyn, New York.

**ABOVE** Fossil of Cladoxylopsid bark.

**ABOVE** The spore-bearing capsules, or sporangia, of Cooksonia, considered the first land plant with a vascular system.

years ago. Unearthed near Prague from stratum dating to the Silurian Period, the fossil is comprised of a forked stem with a trumpet-shaped spore case at its end. Since it has no leaves, the species is believed to have photosynthesized along its stem surface.

The most massive find of all may be the Florissant Formation, in Florissant, Teller County, Colorado, a paleological goldmine. There, 34 million years ago, the area was a lake environment with redwood trees. The trees are now stone stumps, the petrified ghosts of *Sequoia affinis*, a close relative of the modern coast redwood (*S. sempervirens*). Fossil trees in the main Petrified Forest represent Sequoioxylon, a name for fossil wood closely related to the Sequoia. Volcanic eruptions buried the valley and petrified the redwoods, and tens of thousands of fossils have been recovered from the resulting ash falls and mudflows.

> "I observed on most collected stones the imprints of innumerable plant fragments which were so different from those which are growing in the Lyonnais, in the nearby provinces, and even in the rest of France, that I felt like collecting plants in a new world . . . The number of these leaves, the way they separated easily, and the great variety of plants whose imprints I saw, appeared to me just as many volumes of botany representing in the same quarry the oldest library of the world."
>
> —Antoine de Jussieu (1748–1836)

1. An unidentified fossil from the Florissant Formation in Colorado, United States. 2. *Populus crassa*, an ancestor of the poplar tree, Florissant Formation. 3. Fossilized leaves of *Fagopsis longifolia*, a common plant found in the Florissant Formation. 4. A fossil of an ancient *Prosopis* pod, relative of today's mesquite trees.

If we're talking elsewhere in this volume about plants that seem to us to have extraordinary lifespans of, say, 14,000 years, reframing the context of longevity to encompass plants that endured through entire geologic *eras* is simply mind-blowing. Perhaps Alfred Russel Wallace (1823-1913) sums it up best in his *Island Life*, from 1880:

> "Not only does the marvellous structure of each organised being involve the whole past history of the earth, but such apparently unimportant facts as the presence of certain types of plants or animals in one island rather than in another, are now shown to be dependent on the long series of past geological changes—on those marvellous astronomical revolutions which cause a periodic variation of terrestrial climates—on the apparently fortuitous action of storms and currents in the conveyance of germs—and on the endlessly varied actions and reactions of organised beings on each other. And although these various causes are far too complex in their combined action to enable us to follow them out in the case of any one species, yet their broad results are clearly recognisable; and we are thus encouraged to study more completely every detail and every anomaly in the distribution of living things, in the firm conviction that by so doing we shall obtain a fuller and clearer insight into the course of nature."

Petrified redwood stumps on the Petrified Forest Loop Trail in Florissant Fossil Beds National Monument, Colorado.

CHAPTER 17

# QILIAN JUNIPER

*Juniperus przewalskii*

AGE: 1,100 TO 2,230 YEARS

THE TIBETAN PLATEAU is known as the "roof of the world," and more specifically as Qinghai-Xizang gaoyuan. With an area of 970,000 square miles (2,500,000 square kilometers) and an average elevation exceeding 14,800 feet (4,500 meters), the Tibetan Plateau earns the respect of all who visit.

Plants growing in the Qilian Mountains in the northern part of the plateau struggle for survival in bitterly cold winters, short growing seasons, poor or almost nonexistent topsoil in many places, and little rain. Average temperatures are 0.4°F to 9.4°F (18.2°C to -7° C) in January, 41°F to 69°F (5°C to 21°C) in July. A more inhospitable growing zone for plants can be barely imagined. Yet, it is a biodiversity hotspot, with snow leopards, white-lipped deer, wild yaks, and Tibetan gazelle. Vegetation in the Qilian Mountains consists of alpine meadows with vast grasslands and mountain shrubs, wet meadows, marshlands, riverine and lake wetlands, but also scattered areas of coniferous forest, including one notable tree species, *Juniperus przewalskii*, the Qilian juniper. It's an endemic and dominant tree species widely distributed on the northeastern

A Qilian juniper growing out of a sheer cliff face in Qinghai Province, Tibet.

**ABOVE** The native landscape of the Qilian juniper, high on the Tibetan plateau.

**RIGHT (TOP)** The Qilian Mountains rising high behind a fortress in China's Gansu Province. **(BELOW)** *Juniperus przewalskii* leaves and berries, Qinghai Province, Tibet.

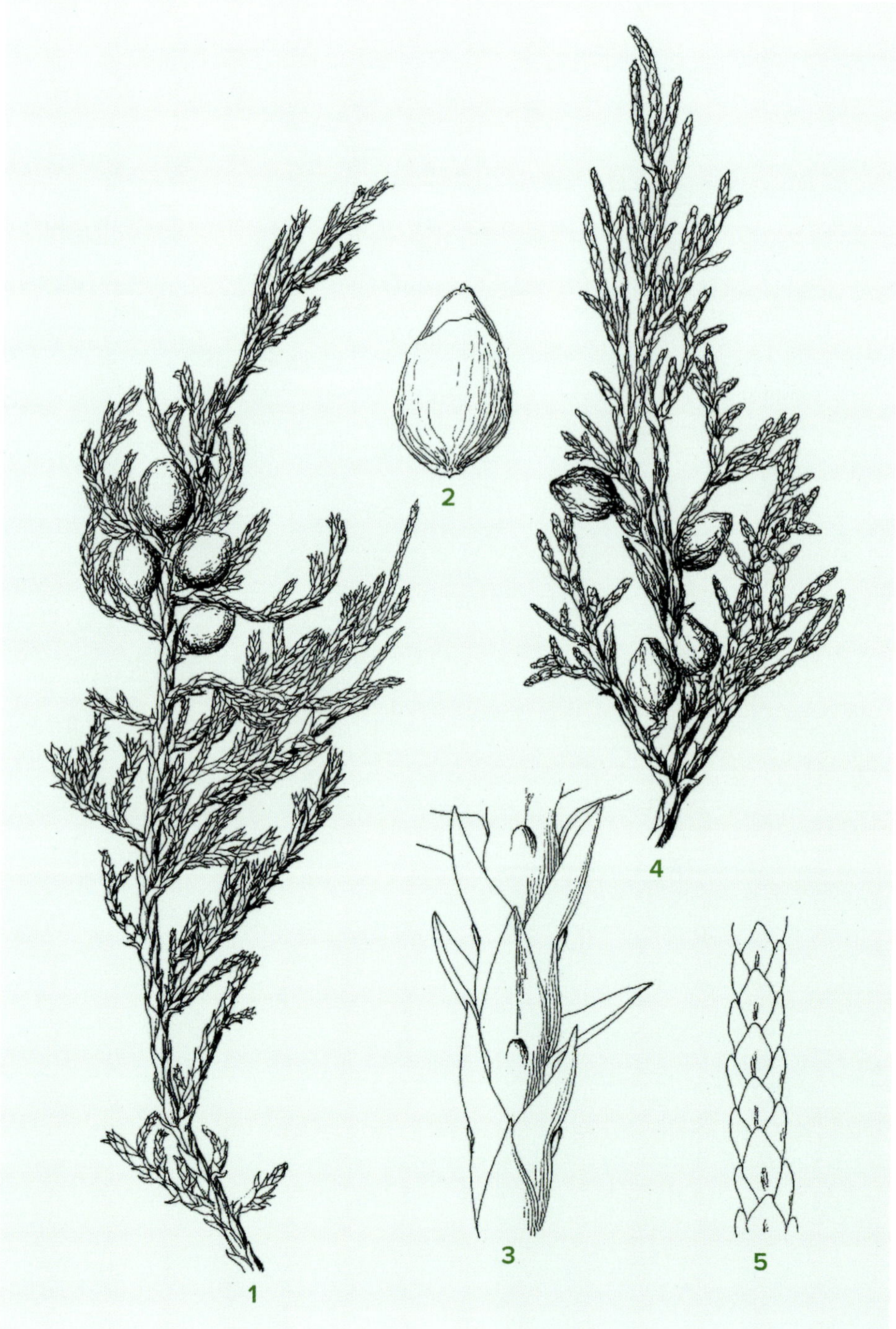

Qinghai–Tibet Plateau that thrives on the dry, infertile southern slopes at altitudes of 8,530 to 14,107 feet (2,600 to 4,300 meters). It is an evergreen tree that manages despite all odds to reach 65 feet (20 meters) tall. The leaves are of two forms, juvenile needlelike leaves, and adult scale-leaves, usually covered in wax.

A 2019 study identified Qilian junipers as being capable of readily living up to 1,100 years old, and 48 trees samples landed in the 901 to 1,100-year-old age class. The study area included the mountains north and northeast of the Qaidam Basin in Qinghai, mostly in the Bayan Shan and Ngola Nanshan. One specimen is reported to be 2,230 years old. Living Qilian junipers commonly reach an age of over 800 years. Living, dead, and archeological wood have been used to assemble a 3,585-year tree-ring chronology, the longest yet developed in China.

As with the bristlecone pines in Chapter 4, we can see evidence here that adapting for slow growth in inhospitable and nutrient-poor environments can be a powerful means of survival.

**FAR LEFT** Botanical drawing comparing two close relatives, the *Juniperus psuedobasina* (1. A cone-bearing branchlet with scalelike leaves, 2. A close-up of the scales. 3. Seed.) and *Juniperus prezwalskii* (4. A cone-bearing branchlet with needlelike leaves and seed cones. 5. A close-up of a branchlet showing more needlelike leaves.). **NEAR LEFT** An old and gnarled, but still living, Qilian juniper growing in the Delingha Region of the northeastern Tibetan plateau.

CHAPTER 18

# REDWOODS

*Sequoia sempervirens, Sequoiadendron giganteum, Metasequoia glyptostroboides*
AGE: 2,070 YEARS+

IT IS ENTIRELY POSSIBLE THAT BUT FOR John Muir and the twenty-sixth president of the United States, Teddy Roosevelt, there would be hardly any redwoods left.

In a now-famous 1920 article published in the *Sierra Club Bulletin*, Muir said:

> "It is often said that the world is going from bad to worse, sacrificing everything to mammon. But this righteous uprising in defense of God's trees in the midst of exciting politics and wars is telling a different story, and every Sequoia, I fancy, has heard the good news and is waving its branches for joy. The wrongs done to trees, wrongs of every sort, are done in the darkness of ignorance and unbelief, for when light comes the heart of the people is always right. Forty-seven years ago one of these Calaveras King Sequoias was laboriously cut down, that the stump might be had for a dancing-floor. Another, one of the nest in the grove, more than three hundred feet high, was skinned alive to a height of one hundred and sixteen feet from the ground and the bark sent to London to show how fine and big that Calaveras

A grove of *Sequoia sempervirens* growing in Redwood National Park, California.

tree was—as sensible a scheme as skinning our great men would be to prove their greatness . . . Could one of these Sequoia kings come to town in all its god-like majesty so as to be strikingly seen and allowed to plead its own cause, there would never again be any lack of defenders. And the same may be said of all the other Sequoia groves and forests of the Sierra with their companions and the noble *Sequoia sempervirens*, or redwood, of the coast mountains."

Thanks to them and others, redwoods are now protected in Muir Woods, Yosemite National Park, and other areas of redwood conservation in coastal California and Oregon.

The three redwood subfamily genera (Sequoioideae) are Sequoia from coastal California and Oregon, Sequoiadendron from California's Sierra Nevadas, and Metasequoia in China. The coastal redwood (*Sequoia sempervirens*) grows along a narrow strip of land from southern Oregon to central California, extending not more than 50 miles (80 kilometers) inland, where it forms pure stands or occurs with Douglas-fir (*Pseudotsuga menziesii*), Lawson's cypress (*Chamaecyparis lawsoniana*), and Sitka spruce (*Picea sitchensis*).

Fog plays a vital role in the survival of these trees, protecting them from summer drought conditions. As coastal fog rolls in from the Pacific Ocean, it condenses on the tall trees' needles, which capture and absorb it directly through stromata; the rest trickles down as droplets to the forest floor and the roots. This intelligent harvesting provides 25 to 40 percent of all the water they need. In ideal conditions, a coast redwood can grow 2 to 3 feet (0.60 to 0.91 meters) annually, but when the trees are stressed from lack of moisture and sunlight they may grow as little as one inch (2.54 centimeters).

Fog at sunrise over Anderson Creek and *Sequoia sempervirens*, protected by the InterTribal Sinkyone Wilderness Council.

Treetop needles are exposed to more dry heat than the needles of branches in the dense canopy below. To compensate for this, treetop needles grow in tight spikes that conserve moisture. The lower branches produce flat needles to catch additional light through the thick canopy.

The trees have shallow root systems that extend over 100 feet from the trunk, often intertwining with the roots of other neighboring redwoods. This increases their stability during strong winds and floods. Redwood is naturally resistant to insects and fungi, because it is high in tannin and does not produce resin or pitch.

Coast redwoods have a conical crown, with horizontal to slightly drooping branches. The trunk is remarkably straight. The bark is very thick, therefore fire resistant, and can be as deep as 1.15 feet (35 centimeters). It's soft and fibrous, with a bright red-brown color.

"Helios" is the name given to the oldest-known coast redwood. It is 375.9 feet (114.58 meter) tall and about 2,068 years old. Helios has also been nicknamed "Mighty Quad" because it is composed of a compressed group of four trunks. Its location is a closely protected secret.

There are estimates that coast redwoods are capable to living to least 3,000 years old, and one estimate of a tree that had lived even to 5,500 years old, but without modern scientific verification.

Sadly, fewer than 5 percent of the original 2 million acres of old-growth forest still exist today.

*Sequoiadendron giganteum* is aptly named. It can grow to be a giant of a tree. In terms of volume, the

**FAR LEFT** The giant sequoia known as General Sherman.

**LEFT** The Grizzly Giant, a *Sequoiadendron giganteum* that's part of Mariposa Grove in Yosemite National Park, California.

world's largest living thing is "General Sherman" in Sequoia National Park. It measures 101.5 feet (31 meters) in circumference at its base, is 272.4 feet (83 meters) tall, and has a total estimated weight of 6,167 tons (5,594 tonnes).

The "Grizzly Giant" in Yosemite National Park is estimated to be between 1,900 and 2,400 years old. It was almost destroyed by a fire caused by a lightning strike in 2003; it's alive but severely damaged. The "Washington" tree is estimated to be 2,800 years old. The oldest living giant redwood is named "The President" and is about 3,200 years old.

*Sequoiadendron giganteum* has awl-shaped, evergreen leaves spirally arranged on the shoots. The seeds are held in cones and released only when the cone dries out and opens from the heat of fire. Its fibrous bark can be 2 feet (60 centimeters) thick at the base of the column-shaped trunk; this also provides significant fire protection for the trees.

Giant sequoia is restricted to a small area of the western part of the Sierra Nevadas, in California. Many are protected in the national parks of Kings Canyon National Park, with over 600,000 visitors per year, and Giant Sequoia National Monument, with 1.3 million visitors a year. Both places are great and glorious cathedrals of trees.

The dawn redwood (*Metasequoia glyptostroboides*) is the third member of the Sequoioideae. It is a fast-growing tree reaching to at least 165 feet (50 meters) in height. The leaves are opposite, bright fresh green, and deciduous, turning red-brown in fall.

Until 1948, most scientists assumed that Metasequoia was extinct, based on fossils from lower latitudes. Then Harvard's Arnold Arboretum received a package from Hu Xiansu, who trained there and returned to China with his doctorate in 1925. In that package were bushels of seeds and

*Metasequoia glyptostroboides* is a deciduous conifer with needles that change color in fall and winter; this grove is on Zhima Ridge in Nanjing, China.

**ABOVE (LEFT)** The seed cones of *Sequoia sempervirens*, which somewhat surprisingly for such a large tree, only measure 0.5–1.4 inches long.
**MIDDLE** A branchlet of triangular, pointed *Sequoiadendron giganteaum* leaves.

other botanical materials, and he documented that they had come from live *Metasequoia glyptostroboides* growing in central China.

Metasequoia is one of the most abundant and easily recognized plant fossils found in the Northern Hemisphere. The plant fossil record provides evidence that the genus *Metasequoia* was widely

distributed and experienced (and survived) a wide range of climatic and environmental conditions from the early Late Cretaceous (100.5 to 66 million years ago) to the Plio-Pliocene (5,300,000 to 11,700 years ago). The modern *Metasequoia glyptostroboides* appears, fascinatingly, identical to its late Cretaceous ancestors.

**ABOVE** The flat leaves of *Metasequoia glyptostroboides*, with immature cones.

Today the genus is limited to one species with approximately 5,000 mature individuals growing in the Xiahoe Valley in southeastern China.

Metasequoia, a deciduous conifer, was also a constituent of the broad-leaved deciduous forests in the polar regions early in its evolutionary history. The trees would have experienced three months of continuous light in summer and three months of total darkness during the winter. This is likely to have given rise to the evolutionary adaptation of losing its leaves during the period of darkness.

Supposedly, the oldest Metasequoia tree in the world is more than 600 years old, and grows in Enshi Tujia and Miao Autonomous Prefecture, Hubei province, China.

Thanks to the world's botanists and horticulturists, the dawn redwood is now widely grown in the temperate regions of the world. It is common in parks and arboreta, favored for its glowing red autumn leaves, its solid winter presence, its soft green spring glory, and its summer luxuriousness, all taking us back to the dawn of time.

It's fitting that John Muir, who did so much to conserve these graceful giants by rallying public support through hopefulness and positive action, should also have these last words describing them:

> "Along the beveled rim of the cañon of the south fork of King's River there is a stately forest of sequoia about six miles long and two miles wide. This is the northernmost assemblage of big trees that may fairly be called a forest. Descending the precipitous divide between King's River and the Kaweah one enters the grand forests that form the main continuous portion of the belt. Advancing southward the trees become more and more irrepressibly exuberant, heaving their massive

*Metasequoia glyptostroboides* is a fast-growing conifer that thrives in moist and even swampy conditions.

crowns into the sky from every ridge, and waving onward in graceful compliance with the complicated topography. The finest of the Kaweah portion of the belt is on the broad ridge between Marble Creek and the middle fork, and extends from the granite headlands overlooking the hot plains back to within a few miles of the cool glacial fountains. The extreme upper limit of the belt is reached between the middle and south forks of the Kaweah, at an elevation of 8400 feet. But the finest block of sequoia in the entire belt is on the north fork of the Tule River. In the northern groups there are comparatively few young trees or saplings. But here for every old, storm-stricken giant there is one or more in all the glory of prime, and for each of these there are many young trees and crowds of eager, hopeful saplings growing heartily everywhere—on moraines, rocky ledges, along watercourses, and in the deep, moist alluvium of meadows, seemingly in hot pursuit of eternal life."

—*The Century Magazine*, August, 1890

**FAR LEFT** The scale of a *Sequoia sempervirens* in Calaveras Big Trees State Park, California, is revealed by the relative size of the walkway below. **NEAR LEFT (TOP LEFT)** In spring, the new deciduous leaves of *Metasequoia glyptostroboides*, the dawn redwood, appear a vivid spring green. **NEAR LEFT (TOP RIGHT)** By contrast, in fall the dawn redwood's leaves change to rusty hues. **LEFT** The trunks of *Metasequoia* can also take on twists and turns with age.

CHAPTER 19

# SACRED TREE OF TAKEO SHRINE

*Camphora officinarum*

AGE: 3,000 YEARS

THIS ENORMOUS CAMPHOR TREE, on the grounds of Takeo-jinja Shrine in Saga Prefecture, located in the northwest of Kyūshū, is the seventh-largest tree in Japan and at 98 feet (30 meters) tall and 65 feet (20 meters) in diameter. The branches spread over 98 feet (30 meters), the trunk is hollow, the inside covering about 65 square feet (20 square meters), or 12 tatami mats. It is said to be 3,000 years old, although this is anecdotal evidence and cannot be scientifically verified as the tree is hollow, making core sampling impossible. There is a shrine to the Shinto god known as Tenjin, the patron deity, or *kami*, of wisdom, scholarship, and the intelligentsia, in the cavity.

Named "Kusu" or "Kusunoki" in Japanese, the evergreen broadleaf white camphor tree (*Camphora*

This 3,000-year-old camphor tree has grown large enough (85 feet/26 meters at the base) for a shrine to have been built directly into its lower trunk. It is the sixth-largest tree in Japan.

**ABOVE** The black fruits of the camphor tree are toxic to humans and mammals, but a food source for birds.

**RIGHT** The crown of a camphor tree at Hirano Shrine in Kyoto, Japan.

*officinarum*) is native to Japan, Korea, Vietnam, Taiwan, and China. The leaves are glossy and waxy and smell of camphor when crushed. In spring, small, white fragrant flowers are produced in abundance and are followed by black berries. Its rough and pale bark is vertically fissured, and the wood is naturally insect repellent.

Camphor is a valued extract of this tree; it's a whitish, translucent substance with a sharp scent, and is made by passing steam through the wood and condensing the vapors. It then crystallizes and is pressed into a waxy form. It is used as a topical medication to relieve itching, and as a decongestant. It is also used as an alternative to mothballs.

The Takeo Shrine is one of Japan's oldest Shintō shrines, first built in 735 CE. Shintō is an indigenous spiritual system to Japan. It is founded in animism, shamanism, polytheism, pantheism, and in the veneration of ancestor spirits. Shintō practitioners believe in *kami*, supernatural entities. These may be male or female, but they reside in trees, rocks, caves, volcanoes, mountains, waterfalls, and streams or exist as natural phenomena such as rain, fire, and even earthquakes.

The Takeo Shrine is located at the eastern foot of Mount Mifune. It is the oldest shrine in the city. The shrine's entrance gate, built in 1641, called

奉祝
天皇陛下御即位
令和

*Hizen torii*, has a unique curved top post and flaring columns. The worship hall is an irimoya-style (hip-and-gable) building with a *karahafu* (curved gable) roof. The color of the shrine pavilion is white to represent the egret, a bird that symbolizes grace, purity, clarity, and simplicity. At the entrance of the pathway to the tree is a *temizuya*, an open area where clear water fills stone basins used to purify one's hands and mouth.

Behind the shrine is a sacred bamboo grove and the camphor tree itself. The trunk is strung with a *shimenawa*, a rope often made of rice straw used to demarcate a holy space, and bearing *shide* (zigzag-folded paper streamers). The wide-mouthed cavity yawns at its base. Much of the tree is hollow, with large upper cavities where two major limbs fell away long ago.

Whatever its true age, its stature gives it a strong spiritual presence, making it no surprise ancient camphors are seen throughout Asia as worthy of veneration. Whether Kusu's is due to the *kami* Tenjin or simply its impressive age, who is to say?

The Takeo Shinto Shrine in Saga, Japan. It dates to the year 735, but the camphor is older.

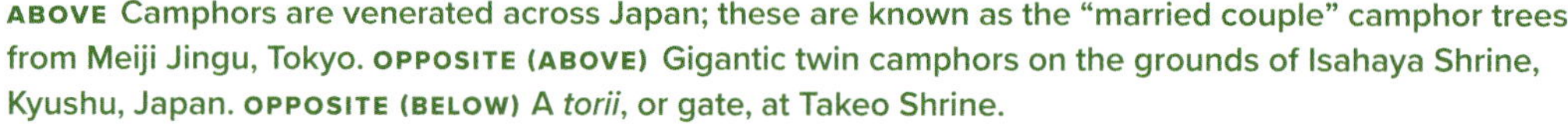

**ABOVE** Camphors are venerated across Japan; these are known as the "married couple" camphor trees from Meiji Jingu, Tokyo. **OPPOSITE (ABOVE)** Gigantic twin camphors on the grounds of Isahaya Shrine, Kyushu, Japan. **OPPOSITE (BELOW)** A *torii*, or gate, at Takeo Shrine.

CHAPTER 20

# SEAGRASS

*Posidonia australis*
AGE: 4,500 YEARS

AND THE WINNER FOR LONGEVITY IS . . . Neptune grass (*Posidonia oceanica*), a seagrass discovered in the western Mediterranean that is 100,000 years old, and possibly 200,000 years old. This makes it easily the oldest known single living plant on Earth.

In 2006, a Posidonia plant about 5 miles (8 kilometers) long was discovered in the Balearic Islands, which was attributed to be 100,000 years old. The plant is located inside a meadow that extends from the area of Es Freus (near Formentera) to the beach of Las Salinas (near Ibiza).

The plant's measured annual growth rate and DNA sequencing indicate the Formentera meadow is between 80,000 and 200,000 years old.

Neptune grass meadows are the homes and feeding and breeding sites of over 100 fish species. Neptune grass forms large undersea meadows in the sands of the Mediterranean Sea, with stems stretching into the sand to form a thick mat of roots that anchor the plant, while bright green ribbonlike leaves grow upward to around 4.9 feet (1.5 meters).

The seagrass meadow off the coast of Shark Bay in Western Australia covers an area bigger than Washington, D.C.

Small green flowers develop into free-floating fruit commonly referred to as "sea olives."

The greatest threat to the survival of these species comes from underwater discharges of wastewater, coastal land reclamation, anchoring and the use of dredging equipment in coastal fishing, and of course increasing sea temperature. The Mediterranean is warming three times faster than the world average, and each year *P. oceanica* meadows decline by around 5 percent.

Another seagrass is not quite the oldest, a mere toddler in comparison to *P. oceanica* at only 4,500 years, but it takes a different prize: largest plant on Earth. This is *Posidonia australis* (ribbon-weed), and it grows just off the coast of Western Australia. The colony in Shark Bay is the largest, spanning 180 kilometers (49,000 acres) of shallow ocean bed.

There are 72 species of seagrass, belonging to four major genera: Zosteraceae, Hydrocharitaceae, Posidoniaceae and Cymodoceaceae. Seagrasses are related to grasses, but they are not true grasses—they are gymnosperms. Their closest terrestrial relatives are actually lilies and orchids. They are the only flowering plants that live underwater. They evolved from life in the ocean, migrated to land, and then back to the sea about 100 million years ago.

*Posidonia australis* has ribbonlike leaves 0.43 to 0.79 inches (11 to 20 millimeters) wide. They start out bright green, then brown with age. It is a monoecious plant, with flowers appearing on spikes on leafless stems. It is found in waters around the southern and western coasts of Australia and extends to the east to coastal areas of New South Wales, South Australia, Tasmania, and Victoria.

***Posidonia australis* covers hundreds of square miles, but its grasses are all one genetically identical individual.**

"We often get asked how many different plants are growing in seagrass meadows. So we finally used genetic tools to answer that," says Dr. Elizabeth Sinclair from the University of Western Australia (UWA), the author of a study on the seagrass published in the journal *Proceedings of the Royal Society*. By sampling seagrass shoots across Shark Bay, also a UNESCO World Heritage Area, the researchers generated a "fingerprint" using 18,000 genetic markers. "There was just one fingerprint among all the samples," says Jane Edgeloe from UWA. "That's it—just one plant has expanded over a hundred and eleven miles, making it the largest-known plant on Earth. The existing ribbon-weed meadows appear to have expanded from one single, colonizing seedling."

To calculate the age of the ribbon-grass, they used the total estimated area of the meadow and divided it by a conservative range of an annual rhizome extension: 5.9 to 13.7 inches (15 to 35 centimeters a year), to get a minimum age of 4,500 years.

Ribbon-weed is a polyploid plant, which means that it has more than one pair of chromosomes. It has double the number of chromosomes of other studied populations (40 chromosomes instead of the usual 20). Most species whose cells have nuclei are diploid, meaning they have two complete sets of chromosomes, one from each of two parents; each set contains the same number of chromosomes, and the chromosomes are joined in pairs. However, polyploidism is especially common in plants.

**ABOVE** Conservation groups have actively been collecting the fruit of *Posidonia australis* to re-seed areas of lost native habitat.

**LEFT** Seagrass provides habitat for conservation icons and charismatic species such as seahorses, as well as many species people enjoy fishing for recreationally.

"Polyploid plants often reside in places with extreme environmental conditions and are often sterile, but can continue to grow if left undisturbed. This giant seagrass has done just that," says Sinclair.

While the combination of polyploidy and clonality have allowed the seagrass to expand into a large geographic range across ecologically diverse habitats, researchers are still surprised it has been so successful. "Even without successful flowering and seed production, it appears to be really resilient, experiencing a wide range of temperatures and salinities plus extreme high light conditions, which together would typically be highly stressful for most plants," she says.

"This single plant may in fact be sterile; it doesn't have a sex," says Dr. Martin Breed from Flinders University in South Australia. "How it's survived and thrived for so long is really puzzling. Plants that don't have sex tend to also have reduced genetic diversity, which they normally need when dealing with environmental change."

The complete set of genes or genetic material present in a cell or organism is its genome. The first plant reference genome, sequenced in December 2000, was that of *Arabidopsis thaliana*, the mouse-ear cress. Since then, more than 1,000 genomes for species from nonvascular to flowering plants have been generated. These growing collections of plant genomes have dramatically advanced studies in all disciplines of plant biology.

Globally, we're losing a soccer field of seagrass, like this *Posidonia oceanica*, every thirty minutes.

Shark Bay, as a UNESCO World Heritage Site, is recognized as a place of exceptional natural heritage and diversity. But all is not well in this ocean. The IUCN lists ribbon-weed as near threatened, while the meadows in New South Wales have been listed by the Commonwealth of Australia as an endangered ecological community since 2015.

Shark Bay is home to more than 10,000 dugongs (*Dugong dugon*), a relative of the elephant and commonly known as the sea cow. Dugongs feed almost exclusively on seagrass and eat up to 110 pounds (50 kilograms) per day. Dugongs are considered globally vulnerable to extinction. The greatest threats are loss of seagrass beds due to climate change, development, and pollution. The loss of seagrass habitat is also linked to rapid declines in fish stocks and subsequent economic losses for fishermen.

Seagrasses also happen to be excellent at absorbing and storing carbon. Globally, seagrasses store 19.9 billion tons of organic carbon. Seagrasses have been declining since the 1930s and are currently disappearing at a rate of 7 percent per year. It is up to us to preserve the oldest and largest plants on the planet.

Shark Bay is such a unique and critical ecosystem it's been designated a UNESCO World Heritage Site.

CHAPTER 21

# TĀNE MAHUTA

*Agathis australis*

AGE: 2,500 YEARS

IN THE KAIPOUA FOREST in the northwest of New Zealand's North Island stands a kauri tree known as the "Lord of the Forest," or Tāne Mahuta (*Agathis australis*). It is estimated to be 2,500 years old and is 168 feet (51.2 meters) high. The Lord of the Forest is not the tallest of its species, but with a girth of 45 feet (13.77 meters), it is the largest in New Zealand. To stand beside it is to experience something that can only be called awesome in the proper sense of the word, to allow its power and presence, so apart from human time and human concerns, to wash over you and reset your perspective.

Another *Agathis australis*, Te Matua Ngahere, known as "Father of the Forest" is not as tall as its neighbor Tāne Mahuta, but it is stouter, with a girth just over 52 feet (16 meters). It is believed to be the second-largest living kauri tree, and to have the biggest girth of any kauri in the country. It is often estimated to be between 1,200 and 3,000 years old. Te Matua Ngahere may be the oldest living rainforest tree on Earth.

The genus *Agathis* belongs to the Auracariaceae family, a family of tall coniferous trees, all but for

Tāne Mahuta is the largest living *Agathis australis*.

a few Southeast Asian species, growing in the southern hemisphere. About 75 per cent of New Zealand is mountainous or hilly, and Aoraki/Mount Cook is the highest peak there, at 12,218 feet (3,724 meters). The Taupo volcano is in the center of the North Island and 26,500 years ago, it produced the largest-known eruption of the past 70,000 years. The fjord-like coastline of the island is 9,300 miles (15,000 kilometers) long. About 15 percent of the land is covered in plants, and 80 percent of those plants are endemic to the country. It is this high rate of endemism plus its geographical isolation that makes New Zealand one of the most interesting botanical countries on earth. Looking to its most iconic plant genera, we can see why: Agathis, Pseudopanax, Cyathea, Dicksonia, Rhopalostylist, Metrosideros, Leptospermum, Nothofagus, and Podocarpus give us clues to why New Zealand is so completely special.

In a Māori creation story, Tāne Mahuta created the earth by lying between Ranginui, the sky father, and Papatūanuku, the earth mother. All the forest creatures are Tāne Mahuta's children—and there are many children in the Waipoua Forest. The forest shelters what remains of the endangered North Island kokako, sometimes called the blue-wattled crow; the brown kiwi; kukupa/kereru the New Zealand wood pigeon; and the very rare kākāpō, a ground-dwelling parrot.

The kauri is a successful species due, in part, to its ability to poison the ground around it. The leaf litter surrounding the trees is acidic, which prevents

Te Matua Naghere is not as tall as Tāne Mahuta, but has a broader girth, at 52 feet (16 meters).

other species of plants from establishing near it, conserving resources for itself. That is not to say that a kauri forest is not abundant—away from the very base of the tree, diverse flora thrive.

The kauri forests contain a rich and profoundly important diversity of plants, and once covered almost 3 million acres (1.2 million hectares), before the first people arrived 1,000 years ago. The first European to sight the islands was the Dutchman Abel Tasman. Captain James Cook made landfall in 1769, and European settlers followed. The kauri forests were subsequently harvested for timber and gum. Clearing for farmland and timber increased up to the mid-twentiety century. Today, the remnant population of mature kauri covers just 18,420 acres (7,455 hectares) and is susceptible to damage from possum and from kauri dieback, a serious soil-borne fungal disease. There is, however, much cause for optimism: conservation efforts are succeeding. Abandoned farms have been turned to regenerating secondary forest and scrubland, and these contain an estimated 148,000 acres (60,000 hectares) of kauri and its associated flora and fauna.

Well-managed timber operations are also contributing to the regeneration. Private organizations such as the Waipoua Forest Trust (a joint partnership between the Forest Restoration Trust and Te Roroa, the Māori guardians of Waipoua), Kauri 2000, and the Puketi Forest Trust are working with the Department of Conservation to establish thousands of kauri seedlings on suitable sites.

**ABOVE** The "Square Kauri," estimated to be 1,200 years old.

**LEFT** The native Waipoua Kauri Forest in New Zealand.

Dense stands of kauri grass (*Astelia trinervia*) also grow in the forest, to a height of 8 feet (2.5 meters) and a width of 6 feet (2 meters). It's often seen with kiokio, crown fern (*Blechnum discolor*) a shuttlecock-shaped bright-green fern. Ferns are abundant, and *Blechnum fraseri* can develop slender trunks up to 3 feet (1 meter) high, while the shiny fronds of kidney fern kopakopa (*Hymenophyllum nephropyllum*) reach to 4 inches (10 centimeters) tall. Mairehau (*Leionema nudum*) is a shrub with scented leaves and white flowers and grows up to 13 feet (4 meters). Hangehange (*Geniostema ligustrifolium*), looking a little like privet, has greenish-white scented flowers and is used by the Māori to flavor meat.

Seen too, is the toothed lancewood, horoeka (*Pseudopanax ferox*), a sculptural small tree with juvenile downward growing fiercely toothed leaves, this and *Pseudopanax crassifolius* are grown by gardeners, which actually endangers it in the wild.

Scattered throughout the forest and growing prominently around the edges are the tree ferns. To say that they are iconic is literal truth, the silver fern ponga (*Cyathea dealbata*) is the symbol of New Zealand, even seen on the uniform of New Zealand's rugby team the All Blacks. *Cyathea dealbata* is a slow-growing tree fern with distinctive silvery undersides to the fronds. Mamaku, the black tree fern (*Cyathea medullaris*) is the most common of New Zealand tree ferns, it is also the tallest, growing

The Waipoua Forest is an important conservation area for many animal species as well, including the North Island kokako and brown kiwi.

to a height of 65 feet (20 meters) and is identified by its black trunk and hexagonal bases of the frond stems. Wheki (*Dicksonia squarrosa*) tends to grow in colonies and grows to 26 feet (8 meters tall). Close to the kauri forest, all three species can be seen growing with extravagance alongside river-banks with another iconic New Zealand plant, nikau (*Rhopalostylis sapida*), the only palm native to the country.

The New Zealand Christmas Tree, pōhutukawa, (*Metrosideros excelsa*) grows along the coast. It's the most colorful of trees in the islands, with bright crimson flowers in late December. One of these, an 800-year-old specimen, holds a special place in Māori mythology: it's said the spirits of the dead descend on the tree into the underworld (Rēinga) to begin the journey to the homeland of Hawaiki. It is a widely cultivated tree but is under threat in the wild from possum (*Trichosurus vulpecula*), and stock browsing.

Mānuka honey is also a forest product, and it may well be the most sublime tasting honey in the world. Mānuka is the Māori name for *Leptospermum scoparium*, a fast-growing evergreen shrub or small tree with oval-pointed leaves, and white or pink, red-centered flowers throughout the year. It and its cultivars are widely grown in gardens, and it is widespread in New Zealand. The honey, from bees that feed on it, is very sweet and rich and is claimed to have antibacterial and immune-boosting properties.

There is hope and abundant life here.

Kauri trees are endemic to New Zealand.

CHAPTER 22

# WELWITSCHIA

*Welwitschia mirabilis*

AGE: 1,500 TO 2,000 YEARS

WELWITSCHIA MIRABILIS is a strange-looking plant by any account. It consists of just two strap-like leaves that look like long, green, thirsty tongues. It is native to the Namib Desert in Namibia and southern Angola, in southwest Africa, and is one of the longest-living plants in the world, with some individuals estimated to be 1,500 to 2,000 years old.

It looks much like a large turnip with dreadlocks and has taproots about 5 feet (1.5 meters) deep that enable it to access any water that might be hiding in one of the most arid places on earth. Its woody stem is cone-shaped, like a large nut, and projects up to 12 inches (30 centimeters) above the ground. The two leaves can grow up to 10 feet (3 meters) and become frayed at the ends. This plant doesn't flower. It is a gymnosperm, like conifers and cycads. The cone-like reproductive organs (strobili) produce nectar that is attractive to pollinating wasps and bees.

There are questions as to how the plant survives in a desert that receives so little rain. Brief morning fog may accumulate on the leaves and be absorbed directly, although botanists are uncertain. The plant is present growing in ephemeral water courses that

*Welwitschia mirabilis* produces pollen cones (pink) and seed cones (blue-green) for reproduction, like conifers.

may receive up to 3 inches (7.6 centimeters) a year, but water in the Namib Desert is never guaranteed. In some years, no rain falls at all.

Welwitschia is a living fossil—112 million years old according to fossilized leafy shoots, seedlings, and pollen. It is one of the most extraordinary plant species on Earth. Shortly after the white person's discovery of *Welwitschia* in 1859 (by the Austrian botanist and explorer Friedrich Welwitsch), Joseph Dalton Hooker of the Linnean Society of London recognized its similarities to conifers and proposed placing the new genus next to *Gnetum* and *Ephedra* in the order Gnetales. Recent gene sequences have validated Hooker's proposal: Gnetum is indeed the closest relative of Welwitschia, and Ephedra is a "sister" to both.

It is now recognized that there are two subspecies: there's *W. mirabilis* ssp. *namibiana,* from Namibia, and the more common *W. mirabilis* ssp. *mirabilis,* from Angola.

The largest known *Welwitschia mirabilis*, thought to be 1,000 years old.

*Welwitschia mirabilis* is most often associated with the perennials *Zygophyllum stapfi*, *Zygophyllum simplex*, *Arthraerua leubnitziae*, *Calicorema capitata*, petalbush (*Petalidium variabile*), butterfly leaf (*Adenolobus pechuelii*), and oakleaf corkwood (*Commiphora wildii*).

In contrast, *Welwitschia mirabilis* is outcompeted by the trees *Vachellia reficiens*, *Senegalia mellifera*, *Vachellia tortilis*, turpentine tree (*Colophospermum mopane*), and sometimes the toothbrush tree (*Salvadora persica*). Among the more frequently disturbed vegetation of larger dry riverbeds, these species and *Welwitschia mirabilis* sometimes coexist, with old individuals growing next to each other, as in the case of the famous "giant Welwitschia," which grows 31 miles (50 kilometers) east of the Namibian town of Swakopmund on the Atlantic coast and is estimated to be 1,500 years old.

Two straplike leaves sprout from a central stem, then the leaves gradually split into multiple segments as they grow, making it look like the plant has many leaves.

CHAPTER 23

# ANCIENT YEWS OF EUROPE

*Taxus baccata*

AGE: 1,600 TO 5,000 YEARS

YEWS ARE SO PREVALENT THROUGHOUT Europe and its collective history that their great ages may be almost taken for granted, in contrast to some of the highly endangered and rare long-lived trees covered elsewhere in this volume. They are a fixture of the landscape, and for good reason.

The European yew (*Taxus baccata*) is notable for bark that turns to gray as it ages. But its dark-green needles are flat and glossy and are arranged in spirals along the stem. Yews are generally male or female but some, over time, change sex. The red fruits are juicy and sweet to birds, who pass the hard and poisonous (to humans) seed through their system, distributing them far and wide.

It is difficult to accurately determine the age of a yew, as very old ones are often hollow in the center, the heartwood typically rotting away. Yews also have the ability to produce basal stems that, over time, merge deceptively into the main trunk.

The Aberglasney yew tunnel in Carmarthenshire, Wales.

**ABOVE** This yew in Fortingall, Perthshire, Scotland, is often claimed to be the oldest-living evergreen in Europe, purported to be 5,000 years old.

There are many claims about the age of many specific "famous" trees, and these are anecdotal. But many of these anecdotes were recorded long ago, giving them great dendrochronological value.

Ancient yews are known as trees of death and resurrection, ruinous feuds and romantic love, solemn magic and poetic delight. They were there when much of the history of Europe was created, are with us now, and are likely to outlive us all.

**ABOVE** The gnarled trunks of the Fortingall Yew as viewed from inside the church courtyard.

Take the Ankerwycke Yew in Berkshire, England. It is believed to be between 1,400 and 2,000 years old. It is growing in the grounds close to the ruins of St. Mary's Priory, the site of a Benedictine nunnery built in the twelfth century. It is a huge and wild tree 26 feet (7.9 meters) in diameter. The Magna Carta, a charter of rights, was signed under this yew on June 15, 1215. It was first drafted by the Archbishop of Canterbury, Cardinal Stephen Langton, to

make peace between King John, son of Henry II and brother of Richard I, and a group of very unhappy barons. It promised the protection of church rights, protection for the barons from illegal imprisonment, and limitations on feudal payments to the Crown. King John didn't want to sign it. He may have been charming during negotiations, but behind the scenes "he gnashed his teeth, rolled his eyes, grabbed sticks and straws and gnawed them like a madman." Neither side complied with the charter after it was signed, and it was annulled by Pope Innocent III, leading to civil war, the First Barons' War of 1215–1217. But the yew was witness.

The charter was signed at Runnymede, a flood plain alongside the River Thames. The yew, now protected by the National Trust, is opposite, on the east side of the river. The tree may have been already eight hundred years old when king and barons pretended to agree with one another.

Legend holds that in 1532, the famously unhappily wed Henry VIII met Anne Boleyn beneath the boughs of that same yew, and possibly proposed to her there. Imagine that conversation. It is estimated that during his 36-year reign, Henry executed 57,000 people (not counting wives). But the yew survived.

This yew witnessed two momentous events in English history: the development of the earliest written constitution in Europe that sought to limit royal power, and a romance that contributed to the rejection of papal authority, the dissolution of the monasteries, and the establishment of the Church of England.

There are many other ancient yews in the British Isles. The Crowhurst Yew grows in a small churchyard in Crowhurst Village, East Sussex, and has

The Crowhurst Yew in Surrey, England, famous for the door fitted onto the tree in the mid-nineteenth century.

been there since before the arrival of William the Conqueror in 1066. It stands in the south of the churchyard, just off a path leading to St. George's Church. It is estimated that to be over 1,300 years old, having been planted around 700. Crowhurst is on the road that leads to where the Battle of Hastings took place and may have witnessed the invasion personally. This yew is female and in 2006, it was measured at 39 feet (12 meters) tall, with a main trunk of 29.7 feet (9.08 meters).

To confuse things slightly, there is also another Crowhurst Yew; it grows in the Surrey village of Crowhurst. While the trees are both of a similar size, they are very different in appearance. The Surrey yew has a door covering one of the openings in the tree's trunk, and is considerably older than its Sussex cousin, thought to be 4,000 years old. This tree is also linked with history: a cannonball from the English Civil War (1642–1651) was discovered lodged into its side.

Like so many ancient yews in Europe, both the East Sussex and the Surrey yews are in churchyards. There are two reasons for this. First, all parts of a yew are poisonous, except for the red flesh of the berry (the aril). The European yew is one of the most toxic species in the genus, followed by the Japanese yew, *T. cuspidata*. Poisonings by grazing of both wild and domestic farm animals are common. Planting yews in churchyards, which were typically walled, protected grazing livestock from ingesting parts of the poisonous tree.

The yew and churchyards have connections beyond the pragmatic, however. Yew trees were usually planted in a deliberate manner: one beside

The yew of Barondillo, in the Guadarrama Mountains north of Madrid, Spain. It is estimated to be 1,600 years old.

the path leading from the funeral gateway of the churchyard to the main door of the church, and the other beside the path leading to the lesser doorway. A priest and clerks would traditionally gather under the first yew to await corpse-bearers. The ruins of Anglo-Saxon churches suggest that the early English planted yews in a circle around churches, which were usually built upon a central mound.

Ancient stories describe the mythological and religious roots of the yew. In Norse cosmology, the world tree "Yggdrasil" is a mythical tree connecting the nine worlds. Although typically translated as "ash," some scholars believe it must have been a yew. In Irish mythology, the yew is one of the five sacred trees brought from the Otherworld. Staves of yew were kept in pagan graveyards in Ireland where they were used for measuring corpses and graves. Staves of yew were also used for carving medieval Irish Ogham letters, for magical use.

The yew was also associated with symbols death and resurrection in Celtic culture, and this theme was, like many other pagan traditions, adopted by the Christians when they began Christianizing traditionally pagan places of worship.

Other specific yews bear specific mention as well. The Fortingall Yew also vies for the oldest tree in the UK. It's set within a churchyard in Perthshire, Scotland. In 1854, it was reported that funeral processions would pass through the arch formed by the split trunk. Another tree vying for the title of oldest is in St. Cynog churchyard in Defynnog,

**LEFT** A page from the Bedford Hours, 1414–1423, showing the yew branch, symbol of the Duchess of Bedford. The coats of arms were overpainted with those of King Henry II of France and Marie de Medici, who later acquired it.

**RIGHT** Though yew berries themselves are toxic, Taxol, derived from the yew, is a renowned anti-cancer drug.

Cymru, Wales. It's a similar age to the Fortingall Yew, but some argue it could be 5,000 years old, making it the oldest tree in Europe.

The ancient yew tree on the grounds of St. Patrick's College, Maynooth, is thought by some to be the oldest tree in Ireland. It could be up to 800 years old, a more realistic claim than that of the UK's trees. It's named after Thomas FitzGerald, Tenth Earl of Kildare (1513–1537), known as "Silken Thomas" (Irish: Tomás an tSíoda), who was said to have played a lute under it before surrendering to Henry VIII, and subsequently being executed.

In northern Spain, in the town of Bermiego, stands the "Teixu l'Ilesia," which in Asturian means "the Church Yew." The tree can be found just outside the village within the precincts of the village chapel of Santa Maria de Bermiego. The giant tree has stood in this spot for possibly well over 2,000 years. Its trunk measures roughly 33 feet (10 meters) in height. But the oldest tree in Spain is the El Tejo de Barondillo, in the Sierra de Guadarrama. It is part of a forest of yews and Scots pine (*Pinus sylvestris*); the lovely stream Barondillo, a tributary of the Loyoza River, burbles over rocks nearby.

In London in the 1950s and 1960s, a particular gesture was widely used: one would raise the first two fingers into a V shape, with the back of your hand facing toward the recipient—it was meant as a strong insult. Where did this gesture come from? One origin story is to do with the medieval longbow, typically made from one single branch of yew.

The longbow had a much greater range, about 400 yards (365 meters), than the French crossbow, and was extremely effective during the Hundred

Yews have a long and intertwined history with lore around death that began with Norse and/or Celtic mythology.

Years War. British archers were so effective with it that if the French captured an English archer, they would chop off the two fingers he needed to draw its bowstring. Bowmen who had not yet been disfigured took to holding up those two fingers to taunt their foes of coming doom. Supposedly.

More scientifically speaking, *Taxus baccata* has had a significant effect on human health. In war, arrows were coated with poisonous yew sap—if the arrow wound didn't kill you, the sap would. Cups and plates made from yew wood would be used to serve any "honored guests" a host might wish to dispatch. Yew has also been used in suicide. In the Gallic wars, Cativolcus, chief of the Eburones, chose to poison himself with yew rather than submit to Rome. When the Cantabrians were under siege by the legate Gaius Furnius in 22 BCE, most of them took their lives either by sword, fire, or a poison extracted from the yew tree. And the witches in Shakespeare's *Macbeth* concoct a poisonous brew from "slips of yew silvered in the moon's eclipse."

The yew's compounds, however, can aslo be turned into powerful life-saving agents. In 1964, a compound from the bark of the Pacific yew (*Taxus brevifolia*) was extracted, named paclitaxel, and used to treat cancer. To meet instant demand, it was estimated the Pacific yew would become extinct within ten years. However, the taxels were synthesized by a semisynthetic route, and research led to the use of *Taxus baccata*, *Taxus wallichiana*, and *Taxus chinensis* var. *mairei* for the drug as well. The taxels have been found to have broad anticancer effects, especially for breast cancer, ovarian cancer, non-small cell lung cancer, and pancreatic cancer.

The tree of death is also the tree of life.

This ancient yew in the churchyard of St. Bartholomew in Herefordshire, England, is fitted with a bench.

## IMAGE CREDITS

Adobe Stock / (c) 2019 Carolyn E. Lochhead: 46–47
Alamy Stock Photo / amana images inc.: 70 top right
Alamy Stock Photo / Anka Agency International: 222
Alamy Stock Photo / Arterra Picture Library: 66–67
Alamy Stock Photo / Askanioff: 72
Alamy Stock Photo / Auscape International Pty: 104
Alamy Stock Photo / Avalon.red: 2
Alamy Stock Photo / Axel Bueckert: 127
Alamy Stock Photo / blickwinkel: 77, 82 top, 105, 155, 185
Alamy Stock Photo / Bob Gibbons: 52–53
Alamy Stock Photo / Botany vision: 68, 71 bottom
Alamy Stock Photo / Brian Jannsen: 130–31
Alamy Stock Photo / British Library: 232
Alamy Stock Photo / Clement Cazottes: 197 top
Alamy Stock Photo / Charles Melton: 54
Alamy Stock Photo / Chris Hendrickson: 94–95
Alamy Stock Photo / Dan Leeth: 168–69
Alamy Stock Photo / Danita Delimont Creative: 42
Alamy Stock Photo / Dave Watts: 100-101
Alamy Stock Photo / David Cobb: 176–77
Alamy Stock Photo / Dennis Stone: 27 top
Alamy Stock Photo / Doug Houghton: 226
Alamy Stock Photo / dov makabaw: 157
Alamy Stock Photo / Edward Parker: 227
Alamy Stock Photo / flowerphotos: 55, 65 top
Alamy Stock Photo / Frank Teigler/ Hippocampus Bildarchiv: 184–85
Alamy Stock Photo / Hans Munch: 148–49
Alamy Stock Photo / Heebphoto: 34–35
Alamy Stock Photo / Hemis: 22–23
Alamy Stock Photo / Homer Sykes: 235
Alamy Stock Photo / imageBROKER.com: 27 bottom left, 48-49, 56-57, 181, 208, 211, 213
Alamy Stock Photo / John Keates: 188-89 top
Alamy Stock Photo / John Steele: 69, 74-75
Alamy Stock Photo / John Swithinbank: 82 bottom
Alamy Stock Photo / Jui-Chi Chan: 196
Alamy Stock Photo / Ken Griffiths: 107
Alamy Stock Photo / Kevin Lang: 152-53
Alamy Stock Photo / Kevin Schafer: 88, 89
Alamy Stock Photo / Lars Johansson: 128-29
Alamy Stock Photo / Layne Naylor: 12
Alamy Stock Photo / lee avison: 126
Alamy Stock Photo / Leonid Serebrennikov: 158-59
Alamy Stock Photo / mauritius images GmbH: 173 top
Alamy Stock Photo / Michael David Murphy: 58-59
Alamy Stock Photo / Nature Picture Library: 40-41, 202
Alamy Stock Photo / Nick Greaves: 26
Alamy Stock Photo / Nigel McCall: 224
Alamy Stock Photo / Panoramic Images: 18–19
Alamy Stock Photo / Peter Elvin: 14–15
Alamy Stock Photo / Peter Turner: 189 top right
Alamy Stock Photo / Phil Degginger: 50–51
Alamy Stock Photo / Philip Scalia: 92 bottom
Alamy Stock Photo / Robert K. Chin: 165 top
Alamy Stock Photo / Ron Emmons: 156
Alamy Stock Photo / Scenics & Science: 90–91
Alamy Stock Photo / Sergey Pristyazhnyuk: 193
Alamy Stock Photo / Sergio Nogueira: 180
Alamy Stock Photo / Steffen Hauser / botanikfoto: 106
Alamy Stock Photo / Tim Gainey: 236–37
Alamy Stock Photo / Ulrich Doering: 24
Alamy Stock Photo / Vadim Nefedov: 150–51
Alamy Stock Photo / Vincent Lowe: 215
Alamy Stock Photo / Wiskerke: 6
Alamy Stock Photo / Wirestock, Inc.: 192
Alamy Stock Photo / YaN: 78–79
Alamy Stock Photo / Yon Marsh Natural History: 228
Alamy Stock Photo / ZUMA Press, Inc.: 80 top
Courtesy Angela Rossen /Sea Grass Network: 203
Courtesy Aomori Prefecture: 71 top
Associated Press / TOPHO: 182–83
Courtesy CSIRO: 118
Dreamstime.com / © Fabian Plock: 221
Dreamstime.com / (c) Hdmphoto: 136–37
Dreamstime.com / © Kareen Broodryk: 27
Dreamstime.com / (c) Karelgallas: 218–19
Dreamstime.com / (c) Khblack: 110–11
Dreamstime.com / (c) Me5640: 30–31
Dreamstime.com / (c) Rmorijn: 233
Dreamstime.com / seaphotoart.com: 205
Dreamstime.com / (c) Yorozu520: 84
Dreamstime.com / (c) Zastavkin: 83 top left
Courtesy eFloras.com: 174
Flickr / Cerryl308: 83 bottom
Flickr / Cesar Garcia: 64 bottom
Flickr / Chris Gladis: 80 bottom
Flickr / Dogtooth77: 114–15
Flickr / Doug Wirtz: 97
Flickr / Forest and Kim Starr: 60, 61
Flickr / Frederic Fontaine: 62–63
Flickr / John Turnbull: 201
Flickr / Natalie Tapson: 102–103
Flickr / Pamela-Ann: 188–89 bottom
Flickr / Patrick Alexander: 98–99
Flickr / randomtruth: 96
Flickr / Rüdiger Þór Seidenfaden: 43
Flickr / Toplu Bilgi: 76
Courtesy Geological Society London/Lyell Collection: 164 middle row
Peter Giesen/Chris Berry: 162
Getty Images / Field Museum: 160–61
iStockPhoto / Almost Green Studio: 140–41
iStockPhoto / CreativeNature_nl: 216
iStockPhoto / Diego Grandi: 93
iStockPhoto / earleliason: 28–29
iStockPhoto / ©Lars Johansson: 124–25
iStockPhoto / Lokibaho: 142–43
iStockPhoto / marat yakhin: 32–33
iStockPhoto / mtreasure: 184 left
iStockPhoto / Nirian: 188 left
iStockPhoto / Norbert Hentges: 25 top
iStockPhoto / Rex_Wholster: 144–45
iStockPhoto / Sam Camp: 38–39
iStockPhoto / Tatsiana Maroz: 146–47
iStockPhoto / w1d: 64 top
iStockPhoto/ Wirestock: 134–35, 186, 206
iStockPhoto / Yeongsik Im: 194
Jim Cheney/UncoveringPA.com: 112, 117
(c) John Luly: 120, 121, 122
Courtesy Kipping Fossils: 164 bottom
Mary Linde: 240
Courtesy Metropolitan Museum of Art / Open Access/ Fletcher Fund, 1956, Object 56.171.4: 133
Courtesy Metropolitan Museum of Art / Open Access/ Gift of Theodore M. Davis, 1909, Object 09.184.216: 132
Courtesy MonumentalTrees.com / Bieuw Roelofs: 231
Nature Picture Library / Dr. Axel Gebauer: 170–71, 173 bottom
Nature Picture Library / Cheryl-Samantha Owen: 25 bottom
Nature Picture Library / Jack Dykinga: 179
Nature Picture Library / Luis Quinta: 65 bottom
Jaime Plaza/Botanic Gardens Trust: 108, 109
Courtesy Proceedings of the National Academy of Sciences / Bao Yang: 175
Courtesy School of Biological, Earth and Environmental Sciences, University College Cork: 164 top
Science Photo Library / Cristina Pedrazzini: 73
Science Photo Library / Geoff Kidd: 85
Science Photo Library / Natural History Museum, London: 167 all
Shutterstock / (c) Adwo: 212
Shutterstock / (c) 2016 Anton_Ivanov: 36–37
Shutterstock / Ear Iew Boo: 190
Shutterstock / Hank Asia: 70 bottom
Shutterstock / Ivan Hoermann: 92 top
Shutterstock / Jacinto Escaray: 86–87
Shutterstock / Kobus Peche: 20–21
Shutterstock / Philip Schubert: 198
Shutterstock / Rafael Novais: 16–17
Shutterstock / Yeongsik Im: 197 bottom
Wikimedia Commons / Agnieszka Kwiecień, Nova: 70 top left
Wikimedia Commons / Bpilgrim: 154
Wikimedia Commons / Kennethgass: 165 bottom
Wikimedia Commons / MUSE Science Museum of Trento: 166
Wikimedia Commons /Nobutsugu Sugiyama, nsp-jp.com: 81
Wikimedia Commons / Sigma64: 83 top right
Wikimedia Commons / Collection of the Staatliche Antikensammlungen: 138–39
Wikimedia Commons / © Stefan Wagener: 172
willemsvdmerwe: 163 all

## ABOUT THE AUTHOR

Christopher Woods began his gardening life at the Royal Botanical Gardens, Kew. He was director and chief designer of Chanticleer, transforming it into one of America's most exuberant, romantic, and flamboyant gardens and made it renowned for creative and innovative techniques. He has served as vice president for horticulture at the Santa Barbara Botanical Garden; director of the Van Dusen Botanical Garden in Vancouver, Canada; executive director of the Mendocino Coast Botanical Garden; and director of the Pennsylvania Horticulture Society's Meadowbrook Farm. Chris lectures widely, including as a keynote speaker at the Northwest Flower and Garden Show, Philadelphia Flower Show, and a variety of public gardens and at private events.

He is also the author of *Gardenlust: A Botanical Tour of the World's Best New Gardens* (2018), and in partnership with UNESCO Natural World Heritage Sites, *Our Natural World Heritage: 50 of the Most Beautiful and Biodiverse Places* (2023).

the politics and practice of sustainable living

# CHELSEA GREEN PUBLISHING

Chelsea Green Publishing sees books as tools for effecting cultural change and seeks to empower citizens to participate in reclaiming our global commons and become its impassioned stewards. If you enjoyed reading *In Botanical Time*, please consider these other great books related to natural history and ecology.

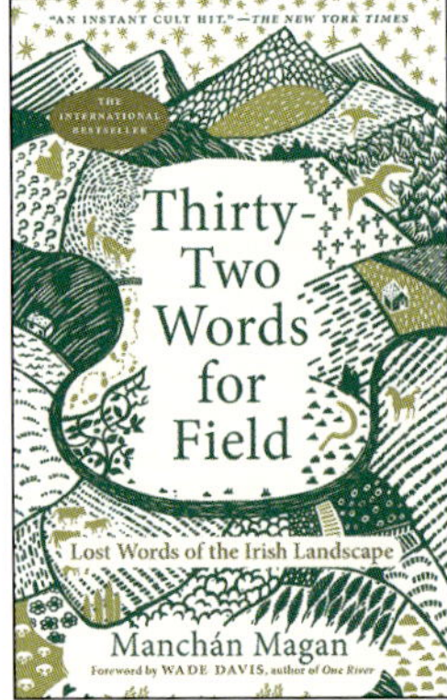


THIRTY-TWO WORDS FOR FIELD
Lost Words of the Irish Landscape
MANCHÁN MAGAN
9781645023760
Paperback

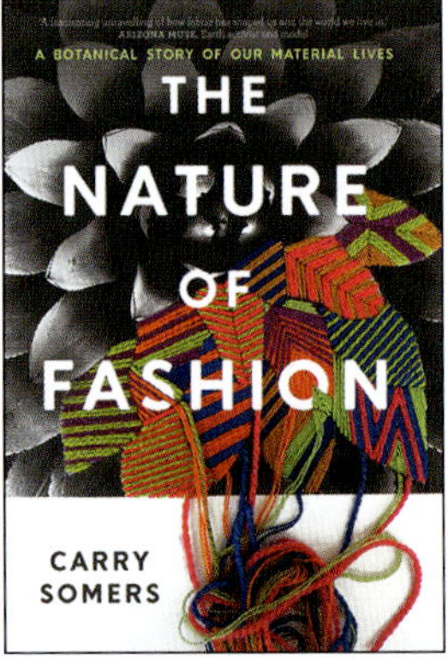


THE NATURE OF FASHION
A Botanical Story of Our Material Lives
CARRY SOMERS
9781915294791
Hardcover

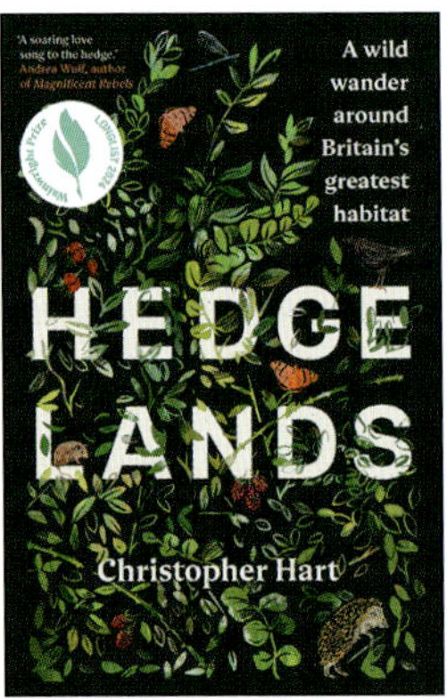


HEDGELANDS
A Wild Wander Around Britain's Greatest Habitat
CHRISTOPHER HART
9781915294470 (US)
9781915294722 (UK)
Paperback

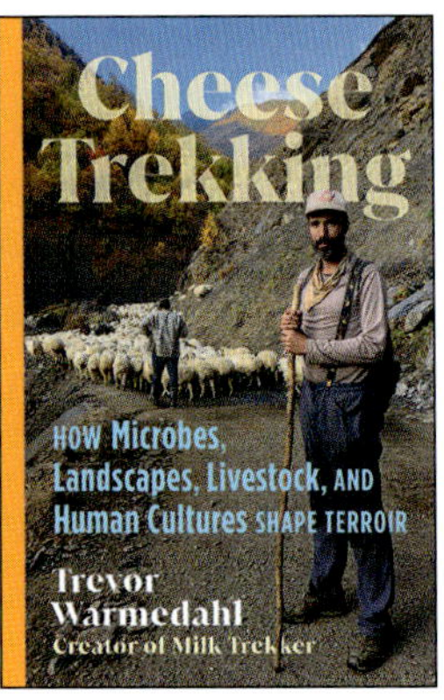


CHEESE TREKKING
How Microbes, Landscapes, Livestock, and Human Cultures Shape Terroir
TREVOR WARMEDAHL
9781645022985
Hardcover

For more information, visit **www.chelseagreen.com.**